The Age of Aquarius II
By
Bobby Legend

Based on a True Story

Legend Publishing Company
33807 Calumet Ct.
Westland, MI. 48186
email: bobwilly81897@Yahoo.com
Tel. #: 734-595-0663
ISBN #'s: 9780982168790

The events, people, and places herein are depicted to the best recollection of the author, who assumes complete and sole responsibility for the accuracy of this narrative.

This novel is based on a true story.

All Rights Reserved © Copyright 2011by Bobby Legend No parts of this book may be reproduced or transmitted in any form by any means, electronic or mechanical, including photocopying, recording, or by any information storage and retrieval system without permission in writing from the publisher.

ISBN #'s: 9780982168790
Printed in United States of America For information or to order additional books, please write to address or tel. # above.

I dedicate this novel to my parents, Francis and Rosemary, my sister Vicky Lynn, and nephews, Billy and Nicolas (deceased) and especially to my good friend and Rock Star, Mickey Strange.

Introduction

Gangsters, Smugglers, Killers: Oh my!

When I returned to my hometown in early 1974, my nightmare truly began. Gangsters and dopers surrounded my life, and my morphine habit was spiraling out of control. However, I made the best of it and continued where I had left off, but on a much larger scale. Instead of dealing kilos, I was now about to deal in tons.

My friend in Europe kept me informed of the progress he was making. He was putting together a very large hash run to America and wanted me to distribute it—all one hundred tons—and I had agreed.

That was just the beginning of what lay ahead. The turmoil would continue nonstop until I left again in 1976 for the country that had kicked me out and that I loved: Afghanistan. My adventures—or nightmares—began anew. May the Lord have Mercy on my soul.

CHAPTER 1

**Landing at Kennedy Airport, February 1974:
Coming Home from New Deilhi, India**

Once off the plane, we weaved our way through the renovation work that was being done. I noticed a bathroom that we could use before reaching the customs area. I could have had ten kilos of hash, cocaine, or heroin on my person and left it in a stall so that one of the workers could have put it in their toolbox and taken it to their department, then put it on their person and carried it out of the airport without suspicion—but that was just a thought. I'm sure, though, that many kilos of dope had gotten into America that way. Oh well, had I known, I might have tried it; that is, if I had known someone who was doing the renovation work to the airport.

So after using the bathroom, splashing a little water on my face, and washing my hands, I was ready to meet the customs man. I just hoped they didn't have my previous history on smuggling drugs into JFK nearly five years before. I knew what to do: stay calm, cool, and collected. I had brought with me valuable hand-painted printed pictures of their "Gods, Goddesses, and Demons," which described their culture from the beginning of their world, and many other tourist gifts worth more than a few hundred dollars for my family members and friends.

I wasn't nervous in any way. After showing the customs man my passport, and him giving me a suspicious look, I showed him my many tourist gifts from my four year expedition, as I called it, and after a few long minutes, without the man saying a word, he handed me my passport and shoved my luggage and gifts to the side. I placed the gifts into my luggage very carefully and I was on my way. I thought to myself, *All right, I did it*. Just then, the customs man called me back to his area. I stayed cool, calm, and collected, hoping it wasn't going to be déjà vu all over again—a customs man taking me into that little room, kicking the shit out of me, and then finding the drugs I had on my person. "You forgot this," he said pointing to a small trinket that I had forgotten to put into my suitcase. I showed my strength, not spilling one drop of perspiration. I left the customs area and headed out the door, into the domestic part of the airport.

Now that I was back in the country that I had promised more than once never to return to again, I was actually happy.

Really, though, I couldn't wait to get home and do some of that morphine I had hidden up my rectum and that hash I had taped to the crack of my ass and down near my pecker, and last, but not least, the Afghani hash I had hidden in my shoes.

Except I had one problem: no money. I didn't even have enough for a phone call. So, after selling a few trinkets to some rich tourists, I bought my ticket to Metro Airport in Detroit and had a little extra for spending money
Nearly three hours after leaving customs, I took what little money I had left and called my mom, telling her I was on my

way home. She was elated and couldn't wait to see me. I couldn't wait to see her, my relatives, and especially my dad and my Armenian grandparents. I was fifty pounds lighter than when I had left and had a hell of a morphine habit, but I didn't care. I just wanted to get home.

During the airplane ride to Detroit, I kept thinking about my morphine. I couldn't wait to feel that rush again…and smoke some of that great Afghani and Kashmir hash.

Before I had telephoned my mom, I had planned to head to Albany to see my Uncle and cousins, to share some of that shit kicking hash with my cousin, Denny, who, in 1968 on our trip from Albany to Santa Cruz, California, had turned me onto my first taste of hash; some excellent red Lebanese. It was a hundred times more potent than the pot that was going around, or so I thought. Much later, I learned that the Columbian mafia, with the help of the CIA, was smuggling tons of excellent gold, red, and blond weed into America: Nearly as good as my hash. Well maybe not that good, but much better than the Mexican weed that was going around before I had left for Afghanistan.

Finally, after an hour or so, I landed at the airport I longed to see. As I traveled through the narrow corridors and into the outer visitors' area, there I saw them: a very large group of my dear family members and relatives. No Willinghams, except for my dad; the rest were from my mother's side: My beautiful Armenian relatives, including my grandfather and grandmother. The only one not there was my great Uncle. His name was Paro, but everyone called him Uncle. I really missed him. Every Christmas, from my childhood until I had left for Europe, I had given him a carton of Pall Mall cigarettes, which he craved. His wife, Nana, who died after being addicted to morphine for 60 yrs., was suddenly taken off of it by her doctor without anything to replace the same drug that I was addicted to. She died from withdrawal symptoms; her heart couldn't handle the loss of the morphine and she died from heart failure. But everyone else was there: My parents, sister, aunts, uncles, and cousins; nearly fifty relatives in all.

We had a great reunion at the airport and continued when we reached our house in Wasteland—Oh, I mean Westland—where they had set up a surprise party. The house was full of my dear Armenian relatives and every Armenian dish you could think of. I liked them all, especially the baklava, a flat or rolled flaky, many layered honey coated nut-filled pastry. After a few hours of partying, everyone left for home. They had all talked about my hash as if I was addicted to it and smoked pipe load after pipe load, as cigarette addicts consume cigarette after cigarette. We all got a laugh out of that, when I told them I had smoked it in cigarette form, not by the pipe load. Actually, I smoked it both ways, to which the Afghans called smoking the "pollen" "pure," before it had been made into hash. They frowned on that, saying, "You go crazy smoking it that way."

As soon as everyone had left, I immediately phoned Mark's mother's house to talk to Mark. He had moved away, so she gave me his phone number. I called it immediately.

Thankfully, he answered my phone call.

"Mark, this is Robert. How ya doing?"

"OK," he said. "How you doing?"

"I'm back in America so get your ass over to my parent's house and bring some 'works'."

He did as I commanded and, within an hour, he was knocking at my door. I answered the knock, anxiously awaiting his presence so I could "do," and let him in. He followed me into the bedroom, after saying "hello" to my parents. Once I shut my bedroom door, I pulled down my pants, gently pulled off the taped hash out of the crack of my ass and grunted out the cigar container holding my morphine. I grabbed a rag and cleaned off the container, then I spewed its contents onto my desk. Nearly 400 tablets of pure, injectable morphine tablets flowed out of it. I turned to Mark, watching as his eyeballs bulged. He slapped me on the back and gave me the hippie handshake.

"Did you get the works, Mark?" I asked him anxiously.

"Yeah," he retorted. "It took me a while 'cause I had to go to Chuck L.'s place to buy them." Chuck wasn't a good friend of mine, just another addict.

"So let's see them," I replied. A few seconds later he pulled out a pack of ten new plastic 1/2cc, 26 gauge syringes, same as diabetics used.

I hurriedly went to the kitchen where my mother was doing the dishes. When her back was turned, I grabbed two teaspoons and returned to the bedroom. Within minutes, after giving Mark two and me three tablets of that evil drug, we were high as kites and, to me, it seemed as though I was back in Afghanistan. However, Mark was having a hard time finding a vein and began spewing half the drug out of the syringe onto the floor.

I yelled to him, "MARK, what the fuck are you doing?"

"I can't find a vein," he said angrily.

"Well, shoot it down your throat. Don't waste it," I exclaimed. "I don't have that many tablets and you're wasting it on the carpet. What the hell is wrong with you?"

He knew what he'd done was stupid, as his faced turned red, embarrassed by his stupid move. He did as I suggested.

I did another three tablets of that powerful drug and was finally at ease, which took away my jet lag.

After ten minutes, Mark was also laid back. It was like old times: Like we were back in Kabul. But then reality hit me: I was back in America. *Oh shit*, I thought to myself. *What had I done?*

My letdown, however, was changed when I opened up the Kashmiri hash that I had taped to my ass. I had thrown it on the top of the desk, along with the stuff I had near my penis area, before struggling to get the cigar tube out of my insides, pushing my sphincter muscle with all my might.

Both pieces of hash were inserted into plastic bags and then taped with a type of duct tape. I undid those two packages with a pair of scissors and out came some of the best hash the world provided.

The room reeked of that age-old smell of Kabul: an aroma only a few Americans had the pleasure to smell. The strong smell of a god-given product: Hashish. Damn good hashish.

The odor was so strong I was worried that my parents would wake out of their slumber, but they had gone to bed shortly after all of my relatives had left. Now it was time to have a little taste of some of that exquisite delight.

My room was still basically as I had left it, so I looked into the top drawer of my dresser and found a hash pipe. I couldn't fill it fast enough. Mark wanted to try the Kashmiri, but I wanted to smoke the Afghani hash, or "Affy," as it was called." We decided to smoke them both: first the Affy and then the sweet, black Kashmiri from the mountains of Kashmir, India. After a few tokes of both, Mark and I were truly laid back.

Mark was too smashed to drive to his home in Detroit, so I asked him to spend the night, which he did.

I definitely had no jet lag left. I was flying higher than a kite. Mark too. Then, I remembered about my shoes.

Leaving India, I had on my person about 8 ounces of both the Kashmiri and Affy hash—but now I was about to open the shoes. I quietly went into the kitchen, got a sharp knife, and returned to my bedroom.

My parents were still asleep, so we weren't worried about them coming in and breaking up the party. I took off my shoes; they were so well made and handmade by my shoemaker in Kabul, who had made all the shoes filled with hash that I had sent to America (besides the envelopes and other items which were used to smuggle hash), so it was hard for me to ruin them. However, the hash was more important than a handmade pair of shoes, so I took both shoes off and, beginning with the first shoe, cut the hand-sewn twine. As I cut, I pulled the shoe apart until I had more than three quarters of it cut. Then the hash spewed out. The room filled with the strong skunky smell of that good old Affy hash that I had been used to for nearly four years.

Now the room reeked even more, so I placed a small blanket under the bedroom door, just to be safe. Nearly a pound of Affy hash had spilled out onto a newspaper I had placed onto the floor before cutting the shoe. Mark and I just stared in ecstasy. This was hash that I had made myself from the pollen I had gotten from the Balk province; the main city is Mazare Sarif. However, the hash plants, *Cannabis indica*, were grown many miles away, near the Russian border, high in the mountains. There, the mujahedeen secured their hectares of plants; usually fifty or more security personnel, each carrying an automatic rifle, such as an AK-47 or a Russian made machine gun or grenade launcher. Those guys were very serious when you visited their territory.

When my friend Tiar and I used to buy hashish in quantity, that's where we would go: the Balk province, to dicker over quality, quantity, and price. Whether we bought hash or not, we always had to pay "Baksheesh" or a tip for their time. Then they would allow us to leave without being shot and or killed. Those days were ones I never looked forward to. It seemed we always had problems; but mostly at the checkpoints, with the police or military, who always wanted their cut of the action, which they called a 'tax'.

The Republicans here in America don't like to use that word, so they call it a fee. God forbid, never speak the word 'tax' unless it's in a phrase such as to "cut taxes." I guess this problem is worldwide, not just in America. In other countries, though, they have no qualms about using the word 'tax.'

After all that hash spilled out of just one shoe, with such a strong, pungent odor, I couldn't believe I was in America with the finest drugs you could find. It was as if I was back in Asia, in a third world country, one of the poorest in the world. The average income was fifty dollars a year. The hash that had come out of my shoe was worth maybe ten dollars in Afghanistan. Here, in America, it was worth 100 times that.

Now I was ready to cut open the second shoe to see how much delicious candy would come out of that one. I was actually salivating as I waited to start the procedure.

Mark was as anxious as I was, so I grabbed the second shoe and began cutting away as fast as I could, until the precious cargo came out: At least another pound or a little more. I figured I had a good kilo and a half of hash, including the 6 ounces of Kashmiri, and at least 400 morphine tabs. The morphine wouldn't last long unless I cut down on my own daily habit. That wouldn't be easy, but I knew that I had to start cutting my number of pills in half or I would run out of my morphine within a month or so. If not, I would start going through withdrawal symptoms that could kill me in an instant. However, tonight wasn't the right time to think about that. When the morph ran out, I would be in deep shit. For the time being, I just wanted to enjoy my "high."

Mark was beginning to get sleepy, but I was still wide awake, just thinking about what I was going to do the following morning.

What a night this was. Actually, I was bummed, having returned to this country, but after smoking the hash and doing 6 tabs of morphine on my first day in America, I was ready to nod off. Mark was already out of it and lying on the bed, fully clothed, snoring up a storm. I lay next to him, toked one more bowl of hash, and that was it for me. I lay the pipe on the floor and shut my eyes, still clothed.

I couldn't wait for the following day. Before nodding off, I was planning my agenda for the next few days, but within seconds I was out of it and fast asleep.

I dreamt about my days in Kabul and thought I was still in my apartment, taking the pollen and making it into hash.

Within seconds of reliving my dream, Mark and I both had awakened at the same time: approximately 10 a.m.

Now I couldn't wait to wash up and visit some of my friends in the neighborhood, especially John C. He had ten thousand dollars from the sale of hash oil that my Peace Corp friend had diverted on his trip to his home in Arizona. My Peace Corp buddy had done me a favor and had gone to Michigan to give my friend the hash oil to sell for me; which John C. had done.

So, Mark and I, still clothed from the night before, went directly to my desk to "do" some morphine before starting out a new day. Mark luckily found a vein and shot up his two tablets, and then lay upon the bed to feel the heavy rush that was traveling through his body. I did the same, but used 3 tablets for my first morning fix. I, too, lay back on the bed to feel that exquisite rush. I couldn't help myself and, within a few minutes, was doing another three tablets of that heavenly drug. After the rush had subsided, Mark and I smoked a bowl of Affy hash and left the house to visit a few friends who had received hash during my stay in Kabul. They weren't aware that I had arrived in America, back in my old "stomping grounds."

We were nearly out the door when the telephone rang. I picked it up. The person on the other end was calling for the airlines, explaining that I had forgotten to pick up my carry-on luggage that contained the knives and forks of the beautiful, handmade and hand-painted paper-mache carving set I had purchased in India, which had nearly got me busted for being a "terrorist. Mark and I used my parent's car and drove twenty-five miles, there and back, to retrieve my carry-on luggage.

At the airport, we walked to the department stated, where a young and beautiful woman handed me my carry-on bags that contained the so called "contraband." I checked out the knives and forks and I was pleased to see that they were in the same condition as when the airline had taken them and put

THE AGE OF AQUARIUS II

them in the cockpit of the aircraft so I couldn't "stab" someone with them.

I thanked the woman and then returned home. I handed the bags of gifts to my mother. Before leaving the house, my mom had a surprise for me. It seemed my dad's old girlfriend, Marge, whom he had met in Australia in WWII, was coming to visit us with her family, which consisted of her husband, two boys, and a girl my age. My mom also told me that Marge's husband was born in Czechoslovakia and had moved to Australia as a child, and in his later years was knighted by the queen, which made him a "Sir" and his wife a "Dame." I wasn't too happy to hear this, but really didn't care. I had more important things to worry about than some guy who had been knighted by the Queen of England.

A few minutes later, I used my parents' car to visit my dear old friends and ones who owed me money, like John C. I carried about a half ounce of some quality hashish with me, to get them stoned as Mark and I were.

First, we visited Joey D., who supposedly had gotten busted by the Feds for the package of boots full of hash I had sent him. I asked him for my collection of albums, but, to my surprise, he refused to return them to me: nearly 500 albums. I left in a huff. I wasn't a hard-ass; I was a pacifist, but I did have other friends who would knock his brains out by beating him to a pulp with baseball bats or who would just plain whack him.

Hours later, I had cooled down and I figured if I had avenged my loss, it would, sooner or later, come back to me. At that point in my life, I didn't need the cops investigating or hassling me. So I let it go for now, but I was going to wait and give him his own surprise when he wasn't expecting it.

My uncle Pete wanted to whack him for me, but I let it go. As a capo in the Detroit Mafia, he told me he would have his bodyguards kick the shit out of him and then bury him on a 100-acre farm, where nobody would find him. I figured it was only material things, even though today my album collection would have been worth at least 6 figures. It was hard to turn Pete down, but once the Mob does you a favor, they own you, lock, stock, and barrel. So, I let it slide. Pete, however, kept calling me to "fix my problem with that piece of shit," but he honored my request and let it go. He told me, "If you ever change your mind, he'll be dead, cut up, and buried where he would never be found." I again rejected his offer.

I told him, "What goes around, comes around. Joey D. will get 'his' when the time is right."

"Well, call me if you ever change your mind."

"Will do."

I was happy that my Uncle Pete was looking out for me and I appreciated that, but, as I stated before: once the Mob does you a favor, they own you. The only way you get a free pass is if you die, they whack you, or you go to some country where you know they're not gonna find you. Although, if they knew where you were hiding and really wanted you snuffed, they would send someone to do their dirty work. To the killers, it wasn't personal…just business.

After Mark and I visited Joey D., we went to see John C, who owed me ten grand for the hash oil my Peace Corp friend, Don, had gone out of his way and had done me this favor. We met in a parking lot across from the Wayne Police Department. I guess John was paranoid and he should have been. He knew what could happen to him if he didn't come up with the green. I pulled alongside his car so that we could speak to each other without getting out of the car, but when he didn't have my money, and worked at United Steel making 500 bucks a week, I was more than pissed off. I was ready to call Uncle Pete, but John nearly cried, giving me excuse after excuse why he didn't have my money. It was mainly because he had gotten a morphine habit from the morph I had sent him along with the hash and he was broke…or so he said. We agreed upon a date when he was to come up with the ten big ones and if he didn't, I told him he would never be heard from or seen again. He knew I meant it.

THE AGE OF AQUARIUS II

After speaking and arguing for more than a half hour, I allowed him to leave, with the promise that he'd have my money within one month. If not, he would be responsible for his own death. He knew I wasn't kidding. Even though he had once been a good friend of mine, this was business and, in business, you either paid your debts or you were gonna end up as fish bait.

We both left the parking lot. Mark and I went to visit other friends that we had grown up with since childhood days. We drove out to Ypsilanti, just a few blocks from where Bill, Sue, and I had lived, together along with my miniature leopard, Kali Durga, which, in Hindu, means: bloodthirsty and more bloodthirsty. Sue and I had looked through an old book of India's gods and demons. We picked the demon side of things.

In the slums of the city, where the railroad station once stood in Ypsilanti, in an old and moldy building on the third floor, was a company called Buzz Co. There, three of my close friends and Joe O, the younger brother of my friend Bill, worked making bongs for smoking weed and hash. They made some great ingenious bongs and wanted to patent some of them, but then thought otherwise, thinking the FBI would close down their business and throw their butts in jail.

After making hundreds of bongs, they would fill up their VW van and go to every pop/rock concert to sell them to the thousands of hippies who used them at the concert or just collected them as collector's items. According to the makers, they made "mucho dinero" and sometimes I would tag along and sell pounds or ounces of Affy, Lebanese, or Nepalese hashish. Basically, I would sell what I had on hand. By the time we returned to our cities, we all had made a nice profit, especially with the different varieties of hash I had sold. On one particular trip I made over ten grand. Buzz Co. sold completely out of their bongs and they too, made a handsome profit, around 5 grand. So, we did this at a number of concerts and were never hassled once.

For instance, at the Goose Lake festival in 1970, I had brought with me about fifty pounds of three different types of hash: Red Lebanese, Nepalese finger, and some of my one toke Affy, black with white streaks running through it. Each was some of the best hash in the world. In fact, I sold out so fast I had to buy a few ounces for myself and friends. Boy, those were the days.

Goose Lake Rock Festival lasted 3 days, Friday, Saturday, and Sunday. However, I had to leave Sunday, mid-afternoon, because my case for smuggling hash into Kennedy airport the following morning was more important than listening to the last few bands. I had to be at the Queens Court House for sentencing. I was sure I was gonna do hard time, but instead I was put on one year's probation and if I didn't get into any trouble for one year, they would expunge the conviction from my record, which they did. However, before my year's probation was completed, I split for Europe with about 700 dollars in my pocket and an open round trip ticket to Morocco. After traveling to Spain in 1967 with the World of Foreign Exchange Students, school wasn't that important to me anymore: traveling around the world was. I made a promise to myself. As soon as I could, I would work and sell hash on the side to get enough money to travel where the best hash was made. I ended up in Kabul, Afghanistan.

Now that I had returned to the good old US of A, Mark and I, along with a few other people, one from the Buzz Co, decided to start a band. We put together a four piece band. I played rhythm, Jim P., who had traveled with me to Afghanistan the second time I traveled there, played drums, Mark M. was on bass and Mark L. was on rhythm and lead guitar. We practiced for a good two months until we had about 40 songs down, three quarters of them written by me.

Then something happened to me. I caught some type of disease, which, according to the doctors, was contagious. They weren't sure what I had until a doctor from Switzerland did a biopsy and told me I had hepatitis B.

THE AGE OF AQUARIUS II

The hospital kept me in quarantine for two months before I was released. Due to my illness, the band broke up. Mr. B., my customs man in Kabul and a good friend, was in Chicago for a week or so and then was going to Nebraska to learn how to run his Department of Communications. I received a letter from him and got his phone number. We talked for hours. He wanted me to travel to Chicago, but I was still very weak and very sick. We also talked about sending hash to me when he returned to Kabul and some of the hash oil I had left behind when the Afghan government gave me four days to exit the country or they'd have thrown my butt in jail. I sure hadn't wanted that, but ended up there anyway.

I was able to send Mr. B. the money that he had asked for and once he returned to Kabul, he promised to send me hashish. However, after receiving a second letter from him, I had two guys from the FBI come to my house and they told me explicitly: Not to contact or have any conversations with him or I could go to prison. It hurt me badly that I wasn't able to answer his letters and phone calls. The last letter I received from him stated that he was leaving with his group for Lincoln, Nebraska. That was the last time I heard from him. I was his son's godfather, so I contacted the Afghan Embassy in Washington, DC and asked about him in 2001. The embassy person told me she knew of Mr. B., but didn't know where he was. They told me to call back in a few months, but I never did. I promised myself in 2008 that I would try again and see if they had heard from him, but now it was June of 2009 and I hadn't yet. I just hoped he hadn't been killed during the Afghan-Russian war.

Before leaving Afghanistan in 1974, he told me he was planning to take his family to Thailand. I just pray to God that he did as he said.

Within a few days after being released from the hospital, I received my first letter from a friend of mine, Gunther, whom I had met in Afghanistan; and another letter from the main man, Rolf, who had bought 90% of the hashish harvest of 1973 in Baalbek, Lebanon.

Baalbek was right on the border with Syria, whose army, along with the militia group Hezbollah, defended the thousands of hectors of *Cannabis indica* hash fields.

Gunther wrote that the plan to send me 100 tons of hash, which I was to distribute and sell for Rolf, was "on." I was to get 50% of the profits and Rolf the other 50%. I had one problem: I didn't have enough people to unload the ships that were about to leave Amsterdam for America. Three ships in all. Each ship would have thirty-three tons aboard.

Now I had to find a way to get the hashish off the ships. I went to my people I had been dealing with for years; many of them were friends who, for years, I had sent hash to from Afghanistan. I could only put together maybe a dozen boats and about the same number of people who had the balls to help me with this deal.

After a week went by, I was in deep shit. I figured I would need at least twenty to thirty 40 ft. or bigger boats and approximately 50 people to get the stuff off the ships before the Coast Guard would pick us up on their radar.

While I was consumed with this large shipment, I was also consumed with another problem. My morphine supply had been depleted and I was buying heroin from the Mexican mafia in southwest Detroit. It was everywhere. Most of the people were selling ounces or pounds, which only had maybe 25% of heroin and the rest was cut with other substances. Although heroin didn't give me the rush I used to get from my pharmaceutical morphine, it did, however, rid me of my withdrawal symptoms. I was also on a methadone clinic, getting a 35mg. per dose daily, and got two days of take-homes on the weekends.

While running around trying to buy grams of heroin and going daily to my methadone clinic, the letters were still coming from Rolf and Gunther. The departure time of the ships was only a few months away. I had to get my shit to-

THE AGE OF AQUARIUS II

gether—fast. I had no time to lose. I still didn't have enough people and boats for that much hashish. Not only did we have to evade the Coast Guard, we also had to evade Customs and the Harbor patrol.

While trying to find people to help me with my hash deal, I had a few bad run-ins with a friend, John J. (we had traveled together to Woodstock) and another who had overdosed on many different types of drugs and alcohol.

The latter person, Russ, was a good friend of mine, who unfortunately was married to the girl I had loved at one time. I had told him that I wanted to take his wife to Asia to score some hash. When he Ok'd the idea, I explained to him that she wasn't only going to travel to Asia, but would also be my sexual partner.

I was up front with him because he and his wife were heading for divorce anyway, and even though they weren't getting along, he, I surmised, was heartbroken. On that Saturday night, he went out and committed suicide by taking downers (reds and yellows), downing them with large doses of alcohol with a friend who had taken him to a local bar.

From what I was told, they dragged him into the house and threw him on the floor, where he lay until early the next morning.

On that particular morning, I got into my car and noticed a bottle of methadone was missing so I drove to his house, because I believed he had stolen it the night he went out and partied. Everyone there was still out from the night before, because I pounded on the door for more than a minute before my friend's wife let me in.

I asked her where her husband was and she pointed to the floor of the living room.

I began to bitch rather loudly (waking everyone in the house) at my friend and when he didn't answer, I kicked him in the side with my tennis shoe. I noticed he didn't move. Then, when I stooped down to shake him, to awaken him, I noticed that his eyes were half open and his body was stiff.

I told his wife, "I think he's dead" and everyone began leaving the house in a hurry. I stayed behind to console the wife and immediately called the police and ambulance. But my friend was dead: had been for nearly 8 hours, according to the EMC person who had checked for a pulse and pronounced him dead.

Within a few days, it was going around that I had killed him. That was pure bullshit. I believe he was dead when his friend he had gone out partying with had dragged his drunken body into the house, and then thrown him on the floor. That was the person responsible for his death, or it was the deceased, himself, who had gone out and got plastered, drank my methadone and was given downer after downer. But I got the blame.

When I went to the funeral home to pay my respects, I noticed everyone staring at me, but his wife walked me to see the body lying heavenly in the casket. After writing my name into the guest book, I left.

Days later, I began hearing rumors about how it was I who had killed him. I just let it go. People in "Wasteland" still believed I had killed him, but I knew the truth. The others just wouldn't admit it. I guess they needed someone to blame and I was that person.

The first trouble came when I was with a friend named John W., who had lost a leg due to a motorcycle accident. We were at a well-known nightclub in Westland when I noticed another friend, whom I had known for a good three years and who had been best friends with the deceased. I walked up to him to say "hello" and shake his hand, but instead got a beer bottle broken over my head. We tussled for a while before being thrown out the back door of the club. We continued the fight in the club's parking lot, just across from the local police station.

Luckily, John followed me. He tried to break up the fight, but was thrown by Ray onto the pavement. During this period in my life, I had borrowed a .22 caliber gun from my

THE AGE OF AQUARIUS II

Uncle Bud and I carried it with me wherever I went. Rolling on the pavement, I grabbed for the gun, which was in my front midsection, and I told Ray that I would shoot him if he didn't stop fighting. Instead, he somehow knocked the gun out of my hand. The gun landed near John's leg. I yelled, "John, get the gun."

He picked it up and yelled, "Ray stop fighting or you're a dead man." Ray wasn't stupid and gave up.

The police eventually investigated the fight and, after everything was said and done, including Ray telling the cops that I had "pulled a gun on him," the police believed that he started the incident in the nightclub by cold-cocking me in the head with a beer bottle for no reason. After John denied that a gun was involved, the police pressed charges of assault and battery and attempted murder against Ray.

About a week later, I was staying at my parents' house and Ray knocked on the door and pleaded with me to drop the charges 'cause they wanted to give him fifteen years in prison. After telling him my side of the story about the death of his friend, he seemed to agree with me that I wasn't in any way at fault over his friend's death. We shook hands and that was the last time I saw him. Years later, I heard he was doing twenty years hard time for selling twenty kilos of pure cocaine to an undercover cop. How stupid can you get?

The second time I had a run in with a so-called friend, whom I had known for many years, it took place at his home.

I had just come back from the doctor's where I used to trade some Thai stick (pot) for a prescription of dilaudid. I immediately retrieved the prescription from the pharmacist, who also had bought pot from me, and after picking up my Uncle Cokie, we drove to Dumbo's place—actually his name was John—and sold him some of my dilaudid. When his older brother Pat gave me the money, I didn't have change, so I left my Uncle there and went to get change from a local drug store.

When I returned, John, Pat and another person, Larry, were all high from shooting up the Dilaudid. When I went into the bathroom to shoot up, Larry came up behind me and put a butcher knife to my throat, while holding me around my stomach with his other arm. I immediately grabbed his arm that held the butcher knife and as we struggled, I was able to get the knife away from him. He fell into the tub, facing me. Now the tables had turned.

I had the knife pointed at his throat as he lay in the tub and I asked him why he had done what he had done. Then I yelled for John, "Help me." I thought John was my friend, but instead of helping, he grabbed me with both arms and was able to get the knife away from me.

I yelled, "What the fuck is going on?!"

John mentioned something about me "ripping him off on a heroin deal," which was pure bullshit. I think he had told Larry this, after Larry had given him money for the heroin and John used the excuse that I had ripped him off. He and I both knew that wasn't true.

In the living room, my Uncle Cokie was sitting in a reclining chair while Larry and I tussled on a couch. Larry, on top of me, hit me in the head with a large crystal bowl and I pretended to be unconscious.

I could hear John ask Larry, "Is he dead?"

"I don't know,"

I suddenly grabbed Larry by the shirt and threw him to the floor.

Pat was holding a hammer near my Uncle so he wouldn't get involved.

As Larry sat on the floor; I stood up and sat in a chair directly across from a window, about ten feet away. I had my handmade suede coat off and held it in my lap.

I asked John, "What do you think your mother would think of what you're doing?"

John's mother was deceased. We had been good friends when she was alive and she used to make John and me delicious food whenever I stayed overnight…usually after we had copped dope and did it in his upstairs bedroom.

THE AGE OF AQUARIUS II

John began answering me, telling me how I ripped him off. I told him that was "bullshit and he knew it." I put my coat in front of me, ran across the room, and jumped through the closed glass window. The coat helped stop the glass from cutting me up, but as I was falling, my head hit a parked car and then the concrete driveway.

As I stood up, my adrenaline kicked in and I ran directly across the street to the city police chief's door and knocked on it with all my strength, screaming as loud as I could. The porch light was burning brightly, so when no one answered, I began walking down the porch steps. I noticed Larry running after me.

I didn't think about the blood pouring from my head and down the side of my face, but about why no one came out to see what the ruckus was about.

As Larry came near, I tripped him to the ground. Then I shouted, "Stop it!"

He refused and began pummeling me with his fists (thank God he didn't have Pat's hammer), so I used my teeth and bit as hard as I could into his right leg, just below the butt area.

He finally gave up and yelled, "Quit biting me." I let him go and he fell to the ground, rubbing his wounded leg.

Seconds later, I took off like "a bat out of hell." I ran to the next street. I saw two girls coming out of their home and asked them, "Please, help me…and call the police," which they did.

When the police finally showed up, I saw my Uncle scurrying away. He didn't want anything to do with what was going on, and I couldn't blame him. He smoked hash and pot, but didn't do heroin or "shoot up" like I did.

The police had an ambulance take me to the county hospital's emergency room (which is now closed down). Before I left for the hospital, I gave a cop my car keys 'cause I didn't want John, Pat or Larry to take anything out of my car 'cause I had a beautiful, handmade 4" by 7" by 3" deep jewelry box in there. The box had silver legs made out of pieces of polished flat stone—lapis lazuli—and between each piece of stone was a thin piece of silver. Inside, it was filled with all kinds of old antique coins, carved items made of lapis lazuli, and other antique items I had purchased in Kabul, Afghanistan.

While I lay on a gurney in the hospital, a cop came up to me, handed me my keys (a different cop than I had given them to), and then read me my rights and told me I was under arrest.

"You're nuts," I told the cop. I showed him my bottle of pills. "This is what the guys were after." I added, "And if you don't believe me, ask my Uncle. He was a witness to the whole affair. I then gave him the name of the trailer park in which he lived.

When I told the cop this, he looked puzzled and stunned. "I'll have to investigate this further." Once he did, they arrested Larry for kidnapping, attempted murder, and other charges.

Pat and John, on the other hand, got a free "get out of jail card" because the city's police chief had known the two brothers since they were small kids.

Approximately 3 weeks after this incident happened, only Larry was looking at jail time—I mean 25 to life. At one time, he had been a friend of mine; not a good friend, but an acquaintance.

When I was finally released from the hospital, I walked very slowly, watching for John, Larry or Pat. When I didn't see anyone around, I took the keys to my car out of my pants pocket, unlocked the driver's door, and put the key into the ignition. I started the car and raced away, slamming my foot to the floor, squealing the tires as I drove away, without any more trouble.

When I reached my parent's home, I noticed my handmade Afghan jewelry box was missing. I looked everywhere for it; under each seat, in the hatchback area, but the box was gone. I figured the cop I had originally given the car keys to was the thief.

I always hated the cops. They believed because they had a badge and power to arrest anyone they wanted that they could get away with anything; including shooting innocent people for the fun of it.

And they do get away with it. All that is done to them is that they're suspended with pay. If a citizen did the same thing, that person would be handcuffed, beaten, arrested, and thrown into jail. Even the cop who did the despicable act would usually get a "pass," promotion, and back pay from the time of his suspension. That's the way the system works.

When the court date came up for Larry's trial, he saw me in the corridor and pleaded with me to "drop the charges," adding, "The cops want me to rat on someone or do hard time."

"Why should I drop the charges? You tried to kill me; not once, but twice. I hope you rot in prison," I retorted, then added, "I hope they throw the book at you."

"I'm begging you. The cops want to put me in jail for life," he whined.

"Please drop the charges," pleaded his mother with tears running down her face. I had met her before a few times. She was a nice lady, especially when I visited at her home.

Even though I was angry with Larry, I was utterly disgusted that Pat and John weren't also defendants in the case. I told Larry that "for his mother, I would drop the charges."

When I was called to the judge's bench, I explained the situation concerning Pat and John and told him, "If they aren't charged, then I want to drop the charges against Larry."

When the judge heard this, he retorted angrily, "Who's going to pay court costs?"

Court costs totaled fifty dollars.

I told Larry, "You better come up with the cash or I won't drop the charges." To Larry and his mother, who were poor, fifty dollars was a lot of money.

I sure wasn't about to pay court costs.

Eventually, Larry came up with the money and was set free. By this time I had moved to a different city to get away from thugs like Larry, John and Pat.

Before leaving the courthouse I told Larry, "I never ripped anyone off."

Larry agreed with me. "I didn't think so either."

That was it. Now I was in a new city, twenty-five miles away from Wasteland.

While all this was going on, I was still receiving letters from both Rolf and Gunther stating the hash run was about to start.

Hell, I had just moved to a small boarding house costing me twenty-five dollars per week.

My mom had bought me a one-year-old "Vega" automobile, which helped me immensely in my hour of need.

The hash would be leaving within a month. It was nearly August; just about the time President Nixon had resigned, and I didn't have enough boats or people to remove the hash from the ships to the smaller motor boats. I still only had maybe twelve people with boats; however, I needed far more.

When I talked to my Uncle Pete about the problem with the three guys who tried to kill me, he desperately wanted to get revenge.

I told him I had a much larger problem.

Pete, though, wanted those three punks whacked and cut up into little pieces and then have their dismembered bodies taken to an Armenian Mafia's pig farm.

Hell, I didn't even know there was an Armenian Mafia. But I would soon learn there was.

So I did something I promised myself I would never do: that was to ask Uncle Pete for help with my hash problem.

2

CHAPTER

Uncle Pete helps me out

Uncle Pete and I discussed my problem; getting 100 tons of Lebanese hashish off the ships onto smaller boats, then the contraband would be stored into a warehouse somewhere in NY City before having it shipped from there to Michigan.

Lebanese hash is called 'sack hash' 'cause the pollen is hydraulically pressed into linen sacks containing approximately 700 or 2,200 grams, then tied and stamped with the farmer's name on one side.

I had a premonition concerning my Uncle and getting involved with the Mob. I was about to get knee deep in "shit" and I knew it, but there was nothing I could do. I was in a bind and Pete was the only person I knew with the connections that could get this project going.

Rolf wrote me just a few days before I had my sit-down with my Uncle Pete and a few of his soldiers. Being a "capo" in the Detroit Mob, he had the power to get enough boats and manpower to help unload 100 tons of hashish and hide it without anyone stealing it; like another crew or family.

We put together a plan, which included the five families of NY City. We would have a sit-down with them and square things out.

"What if we get busted?"

"Don't worry. Everything will work out fine. And you can drive the limousine."

"Not a problem," I replied.

Pete explained how things would work. We would have a sit-down with, most likely, the Gambino and the Lucchese families. The Lucchese Mob was run by a guy named Anthony "Mad Dog" Corallo. Neil Delecroche, the underboss of the Gambino family, would speak for them. If agreed upon, they would get their crews together, with their boats, and be ready by the time the ships left their slips, heading for America.

However, I had a few run-ins with law enforcement before the hash shipment had arrived. Driving my one legged friend, John W., in his 1973 Shelby Mustang to cop some heroin in little Mexico, in Detroit, John bought two pounds of some "Mexican mud," nearly 60% pure, to sell to his people. Driving back to Romulus, MI, taking the I-94 interstate highway, the speedometer wasn't working. I figured I was doing well over 100 miles per hour, wanting to get back as fast as I could so I could do some of the three grams he had given me for driving him, but unfortunately, before arriving at our final destination, we were pulled over by a state trooper. He was definitely a rookie. As he came up to the car, I rolled down the window to ask him "what was wrong." He suddenly reached in and pulled me out of the vehicle, then handcuffed me so tightly that my hands started to turn blue as I sat in the back seat of his cop car.

John was in the front seat, where the cop had placed my wallet, which contained the three grams of heroin. "John, get my wallet and take the heroin." It was placed in a folded piece of aluminum foil, but John didn't listen to me. By this time, my hands were beginning to swell. I began kicking the passenger side door. I yelled, "These cuffs are too tight! Would you please loosen them for me?" However, the cop was too busy searching the Mustang for any illegal contraband. However, being a rookie, he forgot to look in the trunk area. The two pounds of heroin was hidden underneath the tire, sitting in the trunk. As my hands started to turn blue, my yelling fell on deaf ears.

Luckily, a Wayne County Sheriff cop, who had stopped for backup, heard my yelling and told the rookie cop, "loosen his cuffs."

Thank God, the rookie cop listened to the sheriff, an older gentleman with much more experience, and loosened my cuffs. I thanked the sheriff for his help. The "rookie" allowed John to leave with his vehicle, and without finding the contraband, I was on my way to Allen Park jail.

When we reached the jail, the officer searched my person and found a number of ounces of Columbian pot. I had them on me to sell to the Mexicans, but found no one who was interested. We found John's connection and after shooting up to check the pureness of the dope, John paid the elderly Mexican man and hid the stuff under the tire in his trunk. Then we took off and headed for the expressway. Twenty minutes later, I got busted.

When the cop asked me about the pot, I told him I had bought it in Mexican town, which he believed. Back then, pot wasn't a big deal. But when they searched my wallet and found the packet of heroin, I was in deep trouble. I was put in a cell with a young kid who seemed to be on a powdered drug we called PCP. It made you feel like you were rubber, bouncing off of walls.

When the chief allowed me out of my cell and asked me questions about the heroin, I told him, "I got it from John, as a gift for driving him to 'cop' two pounds of heroin." When I told him this, he seemed shocked. I added, "Had the cop who arrested me searched the trunk of the vehicle he would have found he narcotics." This I said to make the rookie cop feel like a jerk amongst his peers for not doing a thorough job of searching the vehicle.

I had gotten off with two years probation because my Uncle Pete used his influence by getting one of the Teamster attorneys, who had gone to school with the judge, plead my case.

Once I left the courthouse I drove to my methadone clinic in Inkster. At the time, I was actually getting methadone from two different clinics. One gave me thirty-five milligrams, the other, 100: The former in Detroit, the latter in Inkster.

In fact, at the Inkster clinic, I usually stood in front of a window and drank the drug in front of the nurse who gave it to me. On one particular day, though, I stood to the side, while the person behind me got their Methadone, and I grabbed an old plastic container used for take homes and poured the narcotic drug into it, then gave the original plastic container to the original nurse who had administered the drug to me: some drug addicts were allowed, after being clean for a month, to take either six doses with them, or a weekend dose.

I thought I had gotten away clean, but as I hopped into my Vega, a black guy came up to my car window and put a gun to my head and took the bottle of Methadone away from me. I begged him not to take anything else, he had the meth, and at this point in time, I had everything I owned inside my vehicle. He did as I requested, but stupid me, went to the Inkster police and told the desk sergeant about the occurrence. He told me that he would investigate the matter and to "come back the next day."

The following day, I went to the Detroit clinic and got my dose and was asked by the nurse if I had gone to another clinic. I didn't lie and told her I did; that nobody said I couldn't be on two clinics. Well, the nurse told me to pick one clinic: Theirs or Inkster's.

After the occurrence at the Inkster clinic, I decided to stay with the Detroit clinic: even though I was getting 100 mil-

THE AGE OF AQUARIUS II

ligrams from the Inkster clinic, I didn't want to run into that guy again, who I learned was a counselor at the clinic.

However, on that particular day at the clinic, I met another white guy named Rick, who lived near my old neighborhood and was also selling hashish. By coincidence, he had some nice blond Lebanese for sale. I showed him my Affy and Kashmiri hash. He wanted to trade two grams of Leb. for one gram of Affy. To make another hash connection, I did as he asked. After taking a few tokes of Affy in my car, we decided to go to his mother's house in Garden City, about twenty miles from my place in Belleville.

After the hassle with Larry, John and Pat, I didn't want to be near those guys. I knew if they harassed me again I would have gone to my Uncle Pete and had them whacked. That was a "for sure."

Rick and I became good friends. He had the house to himself, since his mother was living with some guy she met at a bar.

I told him about the hash deal that was about to leave Amsterdam. He turned me on to a few of the bigger dealers in Ann Arbor, who were into growing their own pot. One of Rick's friends, Bob, was a person that I could sell a few hundred kilos of hash to, as soon as I received it. I only had enough people put together that would buy maybe 1,000 pounds and Pete could sell approximately the same amount, which was only 2,000 pounds. That left approximately 199 thousand pounds to sell. I was about to be responsible for a load of hash that I, alone, could not sell. I definitely needed help.

One month later, the time had come. The three ships were on their way to America.

During this time, I was also being sent 89% heroin from Daniel, my friend in Thailand, whom I had met in New Delhi, India, a year before. Our business only lasted a few months. I had done a stupid thing; I called him by telephone never thinking that we would be "bugged" by Thailand security forces and my own country. The very next time I phoned him, I was told by his friend that he had been taken away by the police for sending heroin to America. I knew he had gotten busted by my stupidity.

I should have known that when the two FBI agents came to my home telling me never again to have any conversations with my old and dear friend from Afghanistan, Mr. B. I was learning fast.

A few days after talking with my Uncle Pete, I drove him and two of his soldiers to New York City (stopping once to refuel) to Mulberry Street in Queens. We rode in a Cadillac limousine, which my Uncle mentioned was once used by Jimmy Hoffa and the Teamsters.

Most of our conversations during our long and boring ride were about James Hoffa and how he had been screwed by Robert Kennedy and how Jimmy, himself, had gotten Pete his job as a Union Delegate for the Teamsters.

I also learned from Pete that Hoffa had been released from Federal Prison just before Christmas in 1971. Pete was really hyped up about Hoffa returning to the Presidency of the Teamsters sometime in 1975. He also mentioned that without Hoffa's help through another associate named "Bobby C," Pete couldn't have gotten me the Teamster attorney.

Now, I was in the great city of New York, and Pete had given me the directions to this small, dingy building on Mulberry Street. I couldn't believe I was about to deal with the Mob, or should I say, my Uncle Pete was having a sit-down with them.

I, along with Pete's soldiers, was told to stay in the limo, while Pete went into a bar-like building called "The Friend's Club." Twenty minutes later, we picked up an extra passenger, introduced to me as Neil Delecroche. Evidently, he was one of two bosses under Carlo Gambino, the real boss of the Gambino crew.

I was given directions to our next and final destination, a small bar in New Jersey. All of the passengers, including myself, were being directed into another small, dingy building. I, along with Pete's soldiers, was told to sit at the bar and have a drink, but I didn't drink alcohol. All I wanted to do was relieve myself. I hadn't taken a piss since leaving Detroit.

Pete, Neil Delecroche, and another person, who I was told was Anthony Corallo, but called "Tony Ducks," and boss of the Lucchese family sat at a small table along with the other boss of the Gambino family, Paul Castellano. It seemed by the gestures made by Neil Delecroche that he wasn't too happy with Castellano being part of the sit-down with Pete and Corallo. After a few minutes of bitching, Delecroche gave up and allowed Castellano to join in on the conversation. I couldn't really hear what was being said, but I knew what Pete was asking them. The talks continued for more than an hour.

While sitting at the bar, I was introduced by Sal, one of Pete's soldiers, to a guy that had come with Castellano. His name was Sammy Gravano. I was also told by Sal that Sammy's nickname was "the Bull." I didn't know if that meant bullshit or a male cow. I found out during our conversation with him that he had been given that name in his early childhood days because he fought like a "bull." But we had a problem, Pete's soldier, Sal, was also nicknamed the "Bull." He, however, got his nickname from being a "bullshitter," not a bull. The other soldier of Pete's who came along for the ride was named Louie. Both of Pete's soldiers were tall and fat. Each one was at least 6 ft. 2 inches and weighed approximately 250 to 280 pounds. When they stared at you, you looked at the floor, not at them. They were called soldiers for one purpose: because they were killers and killing was just business to them, nothing more.

As the four of us conversed, Sammy asked me who I was.

I told him my name and he seemed confused.

"What the hell are you doing here? You're not Italian," said Sammy, giving me a dirty look.

"Sammy, take it easy," said Sal, standing up for me. Willingham's the reason we're here. Pete is Robert's Uncle and he needs some major help in transporting some illegal contraband from some ships coming from Amsterdam and should be here in a week or so."

"What kind of contraband?" asked Sammy.

"Hashish," I told him.

"Drugs! You're in the wrong neighborhood for that, my friend," Sammy stated sarcastically.

"Sammy, Mr. Delecroche has already been told of the situation by Pete's boss, Mr. Giacalone," stated Sal.

"Oh, I see," Sammy said as he stretched out in his seat. Just as Sal ordered a drink, another guy came into the bar. He stopped as he came into the room, looked things over, then walked slowly to us, sat next to Sammy and ordered a whiskey on the rocks.

"Have a seat, Angie" Sammy told the chubby little guy, who was about as tall as Sammy, who was nearly a foot shorter than Sal.

"Ange, what are you doing here?" asked Sammy.

"I need to speak to Neil. I have a message to give him from John."

"What's Gotti want that's so important that you came all the way here from Queens?" asked Sammy.

"That's between me and Neil," replied Angie.

"Angie, let me introduce you to a few of Detroit's finest," said Sammy, as he introduced us to Angie.

Angie asked the same thing as Sammy had. "What the hell is a Willingham doing here?"

Before Sal could say anything, Sammy told him why I was there.

Angie just shrugged his shoulders as though I wasn't there and started a conversation with Sal and Louie. "So you guys are from Detroit, hey?"

"Yeah," said Sal as he stood up, all 6 ft. 2" of him. "We're here to help Willingham with his problem."

"And what problem is that?" asked Angie.

As Sal sat back on the stool, he mentioned something about a hash deal.

Angie gave me the same look as Sammy had—a "cold blooded" look that made me want to be somewhere else at that moment. But when he was told Giacalone had already spoken with Delecroche, he seemed more relaxed.

"You guys know Hoffa?" Angie asked.

Louie and Sal looked at each other before Sal spoke up. "Yeah, we know him," he said. "Pete lives just a few doors down from him. Hell, they play poker together damn near every weekend. It's too bad he was in prison for all those years."

"Yeah, he was put there by a rat," said Louie, the first time he had spoken. He added, "I don't know why the guy's still walking around."

Sal told Louie, "You know why the guy's still alive? It's because Hoffa wants him alive." Louie just shrugged his shoulders and sat quietly from that point on.

Just as Angie was about to ask another question, Sammy interrupted him and asked Angie about his problem.

"How's your case coming along?"

"I don't know?" replied Angie. "My lawyers are looking for a judge to buy. We even asked the Bonanno family, but since Don Bonanno retired, we don't have too many judges in our pockets."

Sammy told him, "You're lucky you're still walking around. If you weren't Delecroche's nephew, you'd have concrete shoes on and be sitting on the bottom of the East River."

Angie didn't say a word and looked at the floor. Then he said, "Yeah, you're probably right. But I'll probably be dead before my case gets to a jury. The doctor's told me I've got the big "C."

I finally got up enough nerve and asked Angie, "What's the big "C?"

"Cancer, you idiot," exclaimed Sal, giving me a look that gave me goose bumps, as if I said another word I'd be the one with concrete shoes sitting on the bottom of the East River.

I didn't say a word. I just turned my head to see if I could see what Pete was talking about with the Mob bosses. At this point, I wasn't too sure if I'd be driving the limo back to Detroit or not. At that moment, I wished I was back in my room at the boarding house in Belleville and had never started this deal. It was much bigger than I had ever dreamed. Now, sitting in a little dark, dingy bar in New Jersey, driving my Uncle Pete and his two soldiers to have a sit-down with three of the biggest and well-known Mob bosses in America was like being in a dream. It was just too much for me to handle.

First of all, I never believed that Rolf would do what he had told me on the plane nearly a year before. Hell, Gunther, who had turned me on to Rolf, was just a poor hippie, or so I had thought when I met him in Kabul.

Just then, my thoughts were interrupted by a loud argument between Delecroche and Castellano. They were both standing as if they were going to fight. Delecroche was more of a thug, while Castellano seemed as though he was a stockbroker or attorney rather than a Mob boss. Or so I thought. After a few minutes of bickering between the two, Castellano gave up the argument and called for Sammy.

"Sammy, let's get the hell out of here," yelled Castellano.

Sammy helped Castellano with his coat and then both walked to the door. Sammy opened the door for his boss, and then both left in a huff.

As soon as both were out the door, Delecroche, still standing, then stated loudly for all to hear, "Castellano is a goddamned business man. He doesn't know the streets. He thinks he's a goddamned lawyer instead of a boss of the Gambino Family."

As Delecroche sat back into his chair, Angie walked over to talk to him, but Delecroche gestured for Angie to go back to where he had been sitting.

THE AGE OF AQUARIUS II

"Can't you see we're talking business, Ange? We'll be done soon and then I'll talk with you," said Delecroche, coughing so badly that we thought we might have to take him to the Emergency room to have him checked out. He chain-smoked cigar-type cigarettes. After nearly a minute of this, he took a handkerchief out of his pocket coat and spit into it, then sat down in his chair to see if he could help Pete help me.

I heard Pete ask Delecroche who Ange was.

I couldn't clearly hear him speak to Pete, but I could tell Delecroche was telling Pete that Angie was his nephew.

In the Mob world, if you "fucked up, didn't obey the rules," you were treated like any other mobster member. They whacked you, cut you up in little pieces, using either a chain saw or a butcher's kit, then either buried you or fed you to the pigs. The latter could devour a person in about two minutes. Sometimes they would put the person's feet into five gallon buckets and fill the buckets with fast drying concrete up to their knees; these were called "concrete shoes." Then, if the mobsters used that tactic, they usually took that person on a boat approximately 50 miles from the docks out in the Atlantic Ocean, shot them dead, or sometimes kept them alive and then dumped the body overboard for "food for the fishes."

"So you're Delecroche's nephew, isn't that what Sammy said?" Sal asked Angie.

"Yeah, so?" he replied, seemingly upset by those words.

"Hey," said Sal. "Don't take it wrong. I just figured you were a capo in your crew."

"No, my pal John Gotti's our crew boss," he retorted.

"Why is he your boss and not you?" asked Sal.

"'Cause Gotti did a favor for Carlo Gambino," stated Ange.

Sal became more inquisitive and asked Angie, "What favor?"

"He whacked an Irish puke that did a hit on Gambino's nephew and John whacked him. Or should I say...was supposed to whack him."

"So why isn't he here talking to Delecroche, instead of sending you? Can't this guy Gotti do his own talking...or is he sick?" asked Sal, sincerely.

"Yeah, he could, if he wasn't in jail," retorted Angie angrily.

"Man, I didn't mean to get you upset. I was just interested. Sammy didn't say anything about Gotti being in jail," replied Sal.

"Wait a minute!" interrupted Louie. "This guy Gotti does a hit and gets time for it? Is that what you're telling us Ange? What the hell did he do wrong? Hell, between me and Sal, we did over fifty hits and never once did time. In fact, we were brought in once for questioning on one hit and then we blamed it on a black guy. He's now doing the time for a hit that we did. Ain't that right Sal?" He looked for Sal's approval.

"Louie, you got a BIG mouth," opined Sal, giving him a dirty look. "But actually, he's right, knock on wood." He knocked on the table top of the bar. "We were never hassled for our hits but that one time, and we each lawyered up. The detectives wanted to close the case, so they blamed it on some small time drug dealer, who just happened to be black."

Angie replied, "Well if you must know, John Gotti's doing eighteen months for involuntary manslaughter. John and me were gonna do the hit, but then Castellano, who's Gambino's brother-in-law, had one of his crew come in on it and he was the guy who actually shot the Mick, right at the bar where we were talking to him, by coaxing him to come out to the parking lot to check out some 14 karat gold cigarette lighters that had fallen off a truck," he said with a wink. "And that's when we were supposed to make the hit." He added, "John had it planned so no one would get busted."

THE AGE OF AQUARIUS II

Man, I was listening to this talk and couldn't believe it. These guys were talking about whacking people as if it was like putting 50 cents in a pop machine. Killing in a war for your country is one thing; you had no choice, and usually it's kill or be killed. But these guys acted like whoever killed the most people would win a prize, as though you were at a carnival. I was getting dizzy listening to this talk and hoped that my Uncle Pete would complete the conference between, Corallo, and Delecroche. I wanted to get out of there as quickly as possible.

Thankfully, after another twenty minutes, I was called to the table by my Uncle Pete.

Sal and Louie also followed me, but Pete let them know what was up. "Sal, Louie, go back to your table and have another drink. We only want to speak with Willingham. This is his deal," Pete told them, as he gestured with his hands for them to sit back down where they had been sitting.

As I walked slowly to the table, it seemed as though I was walking in slow motion, as if I was sleep walking, taking ten minutes to walk ten feet from the bar to their table. Finally, I reached them. Pete kicked a chair towards me, to sit with the top Mob bosses and go over the deal that they had worked out.

Pete introduced me to Tony Corallo, and I had already been introduced to Delecroche two hours before. I just sat in my chair, shaking like a leaf. I was so nervous, I wished I had done three or four tabs of morphine before the sit-down. Once I plopped into my chair, Pete could see I was nervous, because I was literally shaking. Pete noticed my nervousness and told me to "settle down."

"We pretty much have your problem solved," Pete told me. "Mr. Delecroche isn't too happy about helping you with your drug problem. The Gambino Family is against drugs and doesn't allow any of their crews to deal drugs. Mr. Corallo's Family, however, doesn't mind if their people deals drugs: Out of the five Families', only the Gambino Family is against drug dealing. Anyone in his Family caught dealing any drugs is called to a meeting with New York's five families and usually given a death sentence. The other four families don't like selling the stuff, but allow their crews to sell almost any drug you can name. Heroin is their biggest seller. Hashish, however, is a rarity. They'll help you in your endeavor, but only if they get a piece of the pie."

My mouth was dry, but I was able to ask the question, "How much of the pie?"

Delecroche answered, "We'll supply you with the manpower, boats, and anything else that's needed. For that, we want 20%."

"For the 20%, do you want hashish or money?" I asked him.

Pete answered my question, stating, "Money. They don't need the hashish. Corallo might want a ton or so to sell. They're already selling Colombian pot, Cocaine, and Heroin, but Corallo wants either cash, hashish or both. It'll be up to them when the hash is unloaded. Corallo will have to talk it over with his consigliere before he'll know for sure."

"What's a consigliere?" I asked Pete.

Pete replied, "He's a very important person to the boss of the family and gives his opinion to his boss about important matters."

I nodded and then asked, "What if something happens and one or two of the ships get busted by the Coast Guard? That's my main concern. I don't want to get whacked for something I have no control over," I told them.

Actually, I wasn't interested in talking about the shipment. I was nervous not only because of the people I was talking with, but I needed a "fix."

I had brought only a half dozen morphine tablets, two syringes, and approximately 200 milligrams of methadone, but I wanted to "do" the morphine.

I had to be discreet about my addiction. I didn't want any hassles with Pete or the other gangsters. It was Ok to sell the stuff, but not do it. It was a matter of trust. If one of their own got busted by the cops, they might rat on their fellow Family members and bring down the whole Family.

I started shaking so badly that I asked the bosses if it was all right to go to the bathroom. They told me to piss in my pants.

"For Christ's sake, we have important business to take care of," snapped Corallo.

I couldn't put if off any longer. I needed my fix. As cordially as I could put it, I told the guys, "Please, I can't wait any longer. I have to go to the bathroom and take a crap."

They looked at me with scorn in their eyes, but my Uncle Pete said to them, "Yeah, I need to take a break too. I've been sitting in this goddamned chair so long and after the ride in the limo, I could use a break and have a drink."

Delecroche had the bartender bring them some drinks. While they drank their alcohol, I scurried to the bathroom, put two tablets of morphine in my syringe, added some hot water, and shook the syringe until the morphine had turned into a liquid. I took off my belt and used it as a tourniquet around my right arm then went into one of two stalls and shot the evil drug into my vein. Just as I sat back on the toilet seat, Sal and Louie came into the bathroom and jokingly kicked my door, but I had locked it.

Sal told me, "Willingham, you sure got some balls, to leave a sit-down before the bosses were finished telling you their proposition. Had you been a made man and done that in front of the two biggest families in New York, they'd cut your balls off and feed them to you. You're one lucky son-of-a-bitch."

After flushing the toilet and putting my syringe and dope into my front right pocket, I unlocked the stall door and stood behind Sal to wash my hands. Louie had already washed his face and hands, because he was drying them with paper towels that were piled up on one of two sinks in the dirty little bathroom. It had two stalls, two dirty sinks and one urinal and the place smelled of piss. What a place. It was a junkie's paradise.

After I washed and dried my face and hands, all three of us returned to the bar. I think Sal and Louie were just checking me out, to make sure I wouldn't take all day.

When I returned to the table, Pete and the two bosses were sitting there, drinking and bullshitting.

I sat back in my seat and apologized for leaving before we had finished our discussion.

Delecroche and Corallo were the spitting images of real gangsters. They both had very deep voices and were in their late sixties if not in their early seventies. They were the type of persons that wouldn't take shit from nobody. Each carried a .357 or .38 caliber pistol strapped in their shoulder holsters. Pete, Sal and Louie carried theirs in the back of their buckled pants, but theirs were a smaller caliber, like a .25 or .22: The type you carried in case a cop frisked you— he wouldn't feel it.

Delecroche began the conversation where we had left off, before I had gone to the bathroom.

I asked again, "What if something happens to the contraband, such as if the Coast Guard interferes with the shipments or if the ships sink: whatever?"

Delecroche said, "We would take care of that when and if it happened."

That to me meant that they were owed their twenty percent, no matter what happened.

Pete said, "Don't worry about it."

Our sit-down was nearly finished.

"I just want to be clear on one important factor," I told all three.

"And what is that?" asked Corallo. It was the first time he had opened his mouth to me.

I knew he had spoken to my Uncle because I had seen them speaking to each other the few times I turned my head to see if I could hear anything, while I had been sitting at the bar.

Now I laid it on the line. "Mr. Corallo and Mr. Delecroche, if something does happen to go wrong, I sure as hell don't wanna get whacked. And as I said before, I have no control over the Coast Guard, the ships, the ships' captains, or, for that matter, the man who put this deal together."

"And who is that?" asked Delecroche, coughing again as he put his handkerchief to his mouth.

"Sir," I told him trying to stay calm, "all I know is that his name is Rolf and that he bought 90% of last year's crop of hashish produced in Baalbek, Lebanon. I met him by coincidence on the plane flying from Beirut to New York with many stops in between. A guy I had met and sold hash to in Kabul, Afghanistan came strolling through the 747, walking down the aisle, when he noticed me and told me about a guy who I should get to know, who was sitting in first class. So we walked together and he then introduced me to Rolf. And, by coincidence, Rolf had seen me on a European television documentary about the artwork left behind by the tourists from all over the world. The artwork was drawn on the cement and mud walls of nearly every hotel or motel room in Afghanistan. We got to talking and then went upstairs to the bar and main lounge and that's when he told me about a plan that he had and that he needed connections in America. That's where I came in."

Corallo again spoke up. "You're not talking about a guy named Rolf Sandreger, are you?" he asked.

"Yes, I believe that's his name. Why? Do you know him?"

"Know him!" exclaimed Corallo with excitement in his voice. "I got people in Amsterdam that's doing business with him nearly every day: Mostly selling him kilos of Cocaine and Heroin. He's one of the biggest dealers in the world. Hell, if that's the person we're talking about, now I know the situation. The goddamned guy's a billionaire. He practically owns the Netherlands. If you want, I'll have my guy in Amsterdam contact him and, if it's Ok with you, I'll be able to find out exactly when he's having the hashish shipped here."

I looked to my Uncle Pete for an answer. "Sure, why not," Pete said. "Just remember, it's Willingham's deal, no one else's," Pete told Corallo with a cold stare.

"Not a problem, Pete. Willingham's the boss on this deal. We're just back up. But why not let me see what my guy can come up with? It might help," said Corallo, blowing cigar smoke (Cuba's finest) into our faces.

"OK then, it's settled. You can get info from your guy in Amsterdam, but please don't screw up this deal. You got anything of importance to say, you contact me and I'll relay the info to Bob. Understood?" Pete told Tony Corallo.

Pete looked at me for my Ok. I nodded and told the three, "I will tell you guys the exact moment the ships leave. However, if Mr. Corallo wishes to contact his man in Amsterdam, I would rather he didn't. At this time, I don't want Rolf to know anyone else knows about this deal. It could fuck things up," I told them.

I could see Corallo was getting pissed with what I was saying, so I told him, "With all due respect to you, Don Corallo, it's nothing on you. If Rolf thinks the Mob is in on this project, he might think they'll steal the loads and I don't want that. I'm just concerned; that's all," I said. I was just about ready to give him a few other reasons, but before I could speak, Corallo, in his deep gangster voice, showed that he viewed my opinion rather poorly.

"Pete, what the fuck is this little punk saying, huh? That we're gonna fuck things up? We've worked with Sandreger many times. We've been dealing with him for more than ten years. Pete, your little fucking nephew is getting me pissed," exclaimed Corallo, his face turning as red as a tomato.

You could definitely tell he was pissed off. That's all I needed, was to get whacked in this dirty, funky bar before the shit left Amsterdam and then they'd steal it all.

THE AGE OF AQUARIUS II

My Uncle saved the day: he was a Union delegate for the Teamsters and Hoffa's good friend. All Uncle Pete had to do was tell Fitzsimons, the President of the Teamsters while Hoffa was in prison, not to loan their Family another dime for their casino projects in Nevada and other parts of the country.

Corallo got the message loud and clear. "Don't worry kid, I was just trying to make things easier for you, but if you don't want our man in Amsterdam to get involved, he won't. It's as simple as that."

Fuck, I thought to myself. *What have I gotten myself into?*

Suddenly, Delecroche broke the ice. "Ok, Pete. You give us a two day advance notice and we'll have the manpower and boats ready for the pickup. I just hope the seas are calm and not too choppy. Things could get messy and take more time than needed. The longer it takes for us to get the drugs off the ships, the more likely we'll get busted by the Coast Guard. At one time, when Don "Peppino" Bonanno was boss of his Family, we could have bought those guys and wouldn't have to worry about getting busted. But those days are finished. Don Bonanno is now retired and has moved to San Jose, California."

"Well, things are settled then," Pete said to Delecroche and Corallo.

I stood up, then stretched out to shake the cobwebs out of my numb and tired body and shook hands with both Mob bosses and returned to the bar where Sal, Louie, and Angie were sitting.

I watched as Pete kissed both bosses on the cheek, as they did the same to Pete. Even though the two New York bosses had more soldiers and were well known, especially by the FBI, Pete was the one with more clout. He could make them or break them when it concerned loaning them money for their casinos. All Pete had to do was to tell his boss, Giacalone, to tell Fitzsimmons not to loan them money and that was all it took. Even though Pete was only a "capo," he was the top boss of these two bosses we just had the sit-down with. They knew it and so did Pete.

Pete then walked over to the bar and told me, "Bring the limo around so we can get the hell out of here and get back to Detroit." He added, "If you're gonna drive for me, I'm gonna have to teach you how to talk and respect the people I associate with. These guys aren't just some stockbrokers off the street. They go back to the Prohibition days, the days when "Lucky" Luciano was the boss of all bosses."

Gambino was the underboss for Anastasia, who had ordered the Gallo brothers (according to Uncle Pete) to whack Anastasia of "Murder Incorporated" for Luciano and Vito Genovese.

Anastasia was partners with Frank Costello, who was the politician of the commission who had the judges, police chiefs, detectives and many of the police in his "pockets" and, between the two families, was much more powerful than any other family. However, Anastasia did a stupid thing and whacked his boss, Vinchenzo Mangano, without the commission's "Ok." He was one of the original "Mustache Pete's," as Luciano called them, and one of the five families' original Dons.

Anastasia was hit nine times in the barber shop, which he visited daily. That was Anastasia's downfall. He went against the commission's rules. When Luciano heard of this, he ordered the hit and then he backed Gambino to run the family.

Even though Luciano lived in Italy, he was still head boss of the commission and kept things in order. Even after his death in 1962, the commission continued to use "his rules."

Anyone in La Cosa Nostra who killed a fellow member, especially a Don, without the "Ok" of the commission usually was driven to a field and killed on the spot. Before the killing, however, the "rat" was first pummeled with baseball bats and then buried alive. It was a gruesome thing to see.

Thank God I wasn't Italian.

Even so, these mobsters had no qualms about whacking an outsider, even if he was related to a made man.

Now, Pete was responsible for me. If things went wrong with this deal, he, his crew, and I would get whacked. That's the way of the "life."

I had promised myself that "I'd never get involved with the Mob." Now I was knee deep in shit and there was no way to get out. Either they whacked you, or you died unexpectedly.

However, I had a backup plan, just in case. I would leave the country and go to a place where they couldn't find me: Afghanistan. If it was important enough, they could send one of their hitters and whack me there. However, I had friends in the Mujahedeen, who, for a price, would protect me. My passport wouldn't expire for another three years.

Just to be on the safe side, I bought an open ticket to the country that I loved, not knowing if they'd allow me entrance into their country because my passport still had the words written in Persian that I had "spied for the American government." I was determined to return there.

I'd rather end up in an Afghan jail alive than get whacked by the Mob…because I was now under their control.

Before leaving the bar, I took another piss before the long ride to Detroit. Pete was in a hurry to get out of there and ordered me again to get the "fucking" limo. I obeyed and pulled the keys out of my pocket, then walked to the back door where the limo was parked in the alley.

Before entering the limo, I looked all around, praying someone wouldn't come out from behind the dumpsters and whack me. Thank God that didn't happen. I was safe for now.

After unlocking the limo door, I got behind the wheel, started the engine, and pushed the accelerator to the floor. A minute later, I was in front of the bar, honking the limo's horn. Pete, Louie and Sal came out, opened the back door and sat in the plush seats. Pete sat in the seat facing the back of the limo and closest to me, then pounded on the window between me and the mobsters. I used the electronic button to roll the window down and Pete began giving me directions to the New York highway.

"Why isn't Mr. Delecroche coming along?" I asked Pete.

"It's none of your fucking business," he said. Seconds later, he added, "He stayed behind to talk to his nephew, Angie."

"Thanks for your help, Pete," I said.

Pete, being the gangster that he was, answered, "Shut the fuck up and drive."

"We need gas; the tank's nearly empty."

We had driven nearly 600 plus miles and still had a few gallons left over, but we needed gas badly.

Pete handed me his Teamsters Union credit card. "Stop at the next gas station and fill it up with premium."

I did as my Uncle suggested and drove into the first gas station I saw. I stepped out of the limo, opened the locked gas cap with a small key on the key ring and handed the credit card to the gas attendant. "Fill it up with premium."

He did as I suggested, "Nice car," he said, and then looked at the license plates. The guy must have been a psychic because he told me, "You're heading back to Michigan, I bet."

I nodded, and then fell asleep while waiting for the tank to be filled. Ten minutes later, I put the car in gear and headed for the New York highway heading west; stopping at every toll booth through every state but Michigan.

Pete gave me all the money needed to get back to Allen Park. We stopped at different restaurants twice and ate burgers and fries and drank soft drinks. However, on our second stop, coming out of a small out of the way burger joint, we ran into some unexpected flying lead.

As the four of us came out of the diner, Louie opened the driver's door for me and Sal opened the back door for Pete. I was carrying a bag of hamburgers and a few soft drinks and then suddenly a car whizzed by and began firing at us.

THE AGE OF AQUARIUS II

A big white Cadillac, with approximately four people inside, had come roaring by and then did a quick U-turn. Suddenly bullets began flying from the vehicle.
Pete yelled "GET THE FUCK DOWN" but Louie didn't listen. He and Sal took out their weapons and returned fire. Louie was hit in the left upper shoulder and went down onto a rocky driveway. I had dropped the food. Pete, Sal, and Louie, even though hit, fired round after round of shots.

During this time, Pete yelled, "GET THE KEYS AND START THIS FUCKING CAR, NOW!"

I slid over to the driver's seat, staying as low as I could so that I would not get hit. Bullets were flying in my direction. I put the keys nervously in the ignition. The black limo roared to life.

Sal, Louie and Pete kept firing their weapons. Pete opened the back passenger door as wide as it would go. One by one, each slithered into the car. Sal's last shot hit one of the "gangsters" in the Cadillac. Once everyone of our crew was in the limo, Pete yelled, "FLOOR THIS MOTHERFUCKER!"

I slammed the accelerator to the floor with my foot. Ducking down to evade the bullets that were flying from every direction, I drove straight at the Caddy.

The person was still firing his weapon from behind the open rear door on the driver's side when I smashed into it with the limo. I crushed the big guy shooting at us. I believe I killed the guy, because the door sheared off as I hit him and smashed his body against the frame of the car.

We drove away. The guys from the Caddy were still firing their weapons at us, but the limo must have been bullet proof 'cause the back window was shattered but not broken. Once we had a chance to look over the limo, we saw that there were no bullet holes, just some small, round dents where the paint had come off. That was it.

Louie was the only damaged person from that episode back at the diner. He was lucky; the bullet went right through without hitting any major arteries. Sal and Pete evidently had medical training because they patched him up and stopped the bleeding with some paper towels and Sal's undershirt.

I looked into the rearview mirror. I could see three of the guys that had fired their weapons at us checking on their buddy who I had impaled into the frame of the Caddy and who was now flat as a pancake. They immediately threw their buddy's body into the back seat and placed the door, which had come off its hinges, into the trunk of their car.

I was shaking like a leaf and asked Pete, through the open window between the front and back seats, "What the FUCK happened back there! Who would want to shoot us?"

"I don't know. But I'll sure and the fuck find out. Let's forget about it and just drive. What's done is done. Just be thankful that we all made it out alive."

I refused to "forget about it" and asked Pete again. "Why would those guys want us dead? I thought everything had been worked out at the sit-down."

Pete answered my question while Sal was holding the rag onto Louie's bleeding shoulder. "I don't really know, kid. But believe me, when we get back to Detroit, I'll definitely find out: One way or another. Someone might have just started a war; I'll have Giacalone (Tony Jack), Don Zerilli (Joe) or his son "Tony Z." talk to the five families and get this shit straightened out. I think one of the families was pissed off that they weren't involved in on our sit-down." He added, "Whoever it was, they just lost their place in line for a Teamster's loan from its pension fund."

Louie was in a lot of pain. Sal took out a bag of white powder, which I thought was heroin for the pain, but was actually cocaine to numb where the bullet had entered and exited. He placed the coke on Louie's injured shoulder, then he brought out another bag of white powder that I knew was pure heroin, probably made in Thailand. Louie took a few snorts and was out like a light for the rest of the ride.

Eight hours later, we were back in our home state. Only once did we stop for refueling. I couldn't believe it, but this "crate" had two gas tanks and evidently got well over ten miles to the gallon.

Driving back to Michigan, not much was said. Looking into the rearview mirror, I could see Sal and Louie asleep. Pete and I had a discussion concerning the hash run.

"I think we've opened up another door for success," I said to Pete.

He replied, "Yeah, but if we got a war on, then shit's gonna hit the fan. This can't be forgotten. We have to avenge Louie's injury. A quarter inch to the right and it would have hit a major artery and nothing would have saved him. Thank the lord; the bullet went clear through without causing major damage. We'll swing by a doctor I know who'll mend his wounds. Then we'll go to my place and make some phone calls and get this shit straightened out. If not, nobody will get a dime from our pension fund."

I followed Pete's directions to the doctor's place, which was a home not too far from Pete's place.

We knocked on the door and woke up the doctor, and then unloaded Louie. Sal and I dragged him into the doc's place and Pete told him what had happened. We waited until the doc was finished; he stitched Louie's wound within twenty minutes.

The doc gave Louie a bottle of morphine tablets, which I craved. I couldn't wait till I got to a place where I could shoot up.

Nothing was said about the heroin or coke that Sal had given Louie, but as we headed out the door to the limo, I could see Pete counting out a large number of 100 dollar bills, which he then stuffed it into the doc's pocket. The man tried to give the money back to Pete, but Pete would have nothing to do with it.

"Doc," Pete said, "you did me a favor and I won't forget it. Take the money and don't say another word. You earned it. I thank you and apologize for waking you up but we had no choice. Say hello to the Mrs. for me."

A few minutes later, we were in the limo heading for Pete's place. You could tell he was very pissed off, still wondering who the fuckers were who had tried to kill us. He vowed revenge.

3

CHAPTER

Revenge first; Shipment second.

When we arrived at Pete's home, I parked the limo in the driveway. It was 3 a.m. and all the lights in the house were off. The porch light, however, was burning brightly. Pete, with gun drawn, was the first to exit the vehicle, looking to and fro for anything out of the ordinary—like more shooters from the New York area.

When Pete was satisfied, everyone bailed out of the limo. Sal and I carried Louie tenderly into the house, trying not to wake Pete's wife and his two daughters. One from his first wife, was my age and the second, from his second wife, Helen, my mother's cousin, was age 3.

We laid Louie on Pete's living room couch while Sal, Pete, and I sat in opposite chairs and discussed the matter at hand.

Pete was boiling mad about the shooting and wanted revenge against the people who had hit us. At least the tally was one for one. They hit one of ours; I hit one of theirs, who was in much worse shape than Louie. When the limo hit the door of the Caddy, it splattered the shooter like a pancake. If he was alive, it would be a miracle. His legs were nearly cut in half, his head hit the frame of the door and his gun went flying into the air nearly fifty feet from the hand that had pulled the trigger.

After our discussion, Pete made a phone call to Giacalone and then to Don Zerilli's son and told them of our mishap. When Pete finished his phone calls, he told us we had to get Louie home before his wife woke up and began asking questions.

Around 4 a.m. Sal and I loaded Louie into the limo, while Pete stayed home. Within fifteen minutes, Louie was resting on his couch.

I then drove Sal to his house, also in Allan Park, and returned the limo to Pete's driveway, leaving the keys in the ignition.

I unlocked my car door, started the engine, put the transmission into drive, slammed the accelerator to the floor, and got the hell out of there.

Within 45 minutes, I was in my room at the boarding house in Belleville. The first thing I did after turning on the light, and shutting and locking my door, was to get out my morphine and syringe kit. After shooting up, I got the rush I craved instantaneously and lay on my bed until it subsided. I felt as though I was in heaven.

A few minutes later, I was in dream land: Dreaming about my deal with Rolf and my nightmare with the Mob. Even though the morphine put me into a dreamlike state, I tossed and turned all night; thinking about the tons of hash I had to sell, my dealings with the Mob, and about the firefight I had witnessed and was part of. I woke up in a sweat and needed a fix terribly. I noticed then that my morphine was being depleted at a faster than usual pace.

Four-hundred tablets didn't last as long as I had expected it would. Had I been in Afghanistan, I would have done 400 tablets in approximately one month. In America, however, morphine was hard to find.

THE AGE OF AQUARIUS II

I had lost my heroin connection from Thailand because of a phone call. Even though I never mentioned the word "heroin," I did mention that "the stuff was good and send as much as you can, as fast as you can," meaning "every day." That phone call was Daniel's downfall and I never heard from him again after that day.

Daniel, after being expelled for five years from Thailand, had landed in New Delhi, India. His Uncle, who was ambassador to Thailand for the country of Panage, a small country to the west of Thailand, used his power to get Daniel back into Thailand. If Thai security busted him for dealing heroin, they would execute him; that is, unless his Uncle had enough power to get him out of the mess. He had done so when Daniel had been smuggling gold years before.

The reason the military and government officials were allowed to sell the drug was to equalize their money to that of American soldiers.

The typical Thai soldier made approximately twelve dollars a month and the generals made a whopping thirty-five per month, so the king allowed the military and high government officials to sell the "golden triangle's" heroin to anyone with money, especially tourists with many dollars to spend. This was the main reason the monarchy was never overthrown. The government kept running without any interference from Thailand's opposing politicians who wanted a democratic country and not a monarchy. This was especially true of the younger generation of University students. If they protested, the military quickly and fiercely put out the fire, usually by killing their own countrymen, much like MacArthur had done for Hoover when the soldiers from previous wars had protested for the pensions they had been promised. In the American case, as the protesters had gotten closer to the White House, MacArthur ordered his soldiers to fire on them, resulting in the killing of hundreds of America's best. However, the killing of the ex-soldiers brought about utter disgust from the rest of the country, so Congress passed a bill to give the soldiers their rightly due and the pensions they had been promised years before.

In Thailand, the king had little choice: he could either allow the military generals and underlings to sell their most prosperous export or he could face a coup and he, his family, relatives, and close friends would end up dead.

The monarchy had thrived for centuries, if not thousands of years, doing this type of business, as a means of controlling the military and their generals. In the past, however, the main drug of choice had been opium, not it more potent derivative, heroin.

Now I had more problems than that. I was now under the control of the Detroit Mafia. Early the next morning, I was called by my Uncle to have a sit-down with his boss, Giacalone.

That's all I needed. I had no idea what to expect. *Was I gonna become a gangster? Was I gonna have to kill for the Mob?*

All I knew is that I had three hours to get to Pete's house for a meeting that concerned the hash deal and most likely the firefight with the four gangsters. Pete wanted to find out what crime family had done such a foolish thing and who the thugs were, because, without a sit-down with all five crime families, no family was ordered, without the commission's Ok, to kill a made man. And Louie was a made man.

If you were ordered to kill the Vietcong for the US military, that was one thing. But to kill because some guy hadn't paid his vig (interest rate) for borrowing a grand from a loan shark, who in turn paid the Mob a percentage of his gross profit, was another. If that guy didn't pay, he'd most likely end up dead. People who dealt with the Mob therefore usually paid their vig ahead of time. Still, there were plenty of idiots who, if they couldn't borrow the money legally from the bank, got it from the loan shark, who charged one point ($100) per week for each thousand borrowed.

THE AGE OF AQUARIUS II

However, I was in a completely different position. I hoped my Uncle would cut me some "slack." I could still make about ten million if all hundred tons got through and were sold.

If Pete hadn't stood up for me, and if the Mob bosses hadn't known and had done business previously with Rolf, they probably would have kept the contraband for themselves and just said, "Fuck the guy." And they were right. Hell, he was in Amsterdam and Gunther had spoken for me. I was sure they didn't know Gunther. Rolf knew he could trust me. But could I trust the Mob?

And for that matter could Pete trust those New York gangsters?

I believed I could, because my Uncle Pete was very good friends with Hoffa and good friends with Fitzsimmons, the new President of the Teamsters. If the New York Mob fucked Pete, there would be "no million dollar loans to build their casinos in Vegas or a number of other legalized gambling cities."

I awoke very early around 7 a.m., did my fix, and then dressed casually to meet one of the four underbosses, Giacalone, and possibly "The Boss" himself, Don Zerilli. His family went all the way back to the "Purple Gang," and was also very close to the Cleveland Mob, called the "Mel Field Road" gang.

The meeting was set for 10 a.m., so I had plenty of time to get to Pete's house. I arrived a half hour early.

I parked on the street across from Pete's house and locked up the Vega. That really wasn't necessary because Pete was the "Boss" of his neighborhood and if anyone was caught stealing or doing anything against "the rules," they simply "disappeared," usually the same day, never to be seen again.

As I walked up the stairs to the house, I wondered just what I was getting myself into. I had asked the "Mob" for a favor. Now they owned me. There was no doubt of that in my mind.

I nervously knocked on the front door. I felt as though I was going to piss my pants.

Helen answered the door and let me enter. She gave me a big hug and said, "Pete is waiting for you in the living room. And if he asks, tell him that I'm going to visit my sister in Dearborn." With that said, she left, shutting the door behind her.

I slowly walked into the living room. It seemed to take hours instead of seconds. I saw Sal sitting on the couch and two men sitting around a beautiful round maple table. I noticed Louie wasn't there and surmised he was at home, mending his wounds.

Pete motioned for me to come closer to him. He stood up and, pointing to the man sitting at the table, said, "Robert Willingham, I want you to meet one of the underbosses of our boss Don Zerilli: Mr. Anthony Jack Giacalone. We call him Tony Jack or Jack for short, but you'll call him Mr. Giacalone."

We shook hands and I nervously blurted out, "Nice to meet you, Mr. Giacalone."

This guy looked tough, rough, strong, and very serious. You sensed that nobody messed with him unless they wanted to end up "dead."

Our hands separated. Pete then took me a few steps away from the table and gave me a "talking down."

"Listen kid, I'm only gonna say it once. I've vouched for you, which means you're under my protection. And anything that happens to you is my responsibility. You get me?!"

"Don't worry, Uncle Pete, I won't fuck things up. You do all the talking and I'll just sit and listen," I told him nervously.

"Just shut the fuck up and listen! You are my nephew. In fact, because I don't have a son, you're like my own kid. Even though my wife and your mother are cousins, I still feel like you're my own kid or I wouldn't be doing all of this shit for you. Do you get me?"

Pete said this in a way that sent a tingling up my spine, so badly I wished I had never gotten involved with him, his crew, and his Mob, especially Mr. Giacalone.

"Tony Jack" suddenly interrupted Pete's swan song to me and said to Pete, "That's enough bullshit! Now let's get down to serious business and discuss when this shipment is to arrive…and where, so we'll be able to coordinate the offloading of the dope from the ships leaving Amsterdam to our boats leaving from New York Harbor and possibly some from New Jersey." He then kicked out a chair and told Pete and me to "come and sit down."

Pete sat in the chair that Giacalone had pushed out with his foot and I grabbed the other chair directly across from the "boss." Pete was to my right; I sat down and pulled my chair closer to the table and remained silent.

I figured it was better to remain silent than to put a foot in my mouth. One wrong word and a snap of "Tony Jack's" finger, and I could be wearing concrete shoes and shoved into the Detroit River. Hell, I was too nervous to say anything anyway.

With just one look at Giacalone, I knew he was a cold-blooded killer.

Now I was beginning to worry that I would be asked to be HIS driver. The next step would be an order to kill. I knew now that I owed them; not just in money and drugs—but with my life.

I was in a "Catch 22." If I didn't do as they asked, I was "fucked." And if I did do as they asked, I was "fucked." So what could I do, but to sit and listen?

And "Tony Jack" had much to say. It seemed to me that he wanted to take charge of this deal, to cut me out completely. And what could I do if he did? Absolutely nothing.

And if that were to happen, both Rolf and I would end up with "Nada," nothing. And 2 to 1, I would end up dead or missing.

Believe me, sitting at that table made me nervous and dumbstruck, listening to a murderer and cold-blooded killer.

I knew then that I had to speak up and take charge of the situation or something would happen that I wouldn't like—such as ending up dead. I couldn't get that out of my mind. I was in a near trance-like state when I got up the nerve to speak.

I looked "Tony Jack" straight in the eyes and said, "Excuse me, Mr. Giacalone for what I'm about to say, and please, dear God, don't take this wrong, because I'm definitely indebted to you and my Uncle Pete for all your help in putting this through, but it's MY DEAL!" My knees buckled as I stated those last two words. It took all my strength to stay standing, so I planted my palms onto the table to keep myself upright and I continued speaking.

"Mr. Giacalone, you and the New York crew will get your percentage, but it's still My Deal!" Waiting for Mr. Giacalone's answer, I bit my bottom lip so hard it started to bleed.

"Hey, Petey Boy, get your nephew a Kleenex. His lip's bleeding."

My Uncle Pete saw the blood, threw me his handkerchief and said, "Wipe the blood off your lip."

Once I completed that task, Mr. Giacalone gave me some comfort by saying, "Don't worry, kid. You're all right in my book. The way you drove that limo to get you guys out of a double-cross— well, let's just say—you've got a lot of balls. And from what your Uncle told me about that situation, you left one of those cocksuckers flat as a pancake." He then added, "Sure, it's your deal. Hell, for your age, you'd be a good earner that is if you were in Petey's crew. But you're not Italian, although you act Italian under pressure. So, let's just say you're an associate of your Uncle Pete. Understand?!"

"Yes sir, and thank you, Mr. Giacalone. I appreciate that. And I promise you…I won't let you or my Uncle down. I just hope everything comes out as planned. I have my people ready to buy a large quantity of the hashish. And hopefully, before the dope arrives, I'll have many more people to sell the hash to. So, between my people and yours, we should have the stuff sold within a week or so. At least that's what I'm hoping." I hesitated for a few seconds, and then asked, "Do we have the transportation to bring enough of the dope to distribute to my guys?"

"I have a place to warehouse it and secure it. I don't want ANYONE to steal it and then we all lose," Pete stated.

Sweat poured down the sides of my face. I wiped it off with my shirt sleeves.

"Don't worry, kid," said Mr. Giacalone. "We'll have enough people packed and ready to shoot and kill anyone who tries messing with our load. And that goes for the warehouse in Queens. If anyone fucks with us, they'll end up dead and six feet under." He stood up. "Well, Petey Boy, I think we've said everything needed to be said. You just make sure your nephew tells us a day or two before the arrival of the ships."

With that said, my Uncle Pete helped Mr. Giacalone with his coat. Within a few minutes, he had left the house.

Boy, was I relieved. Ten minutes after "Tony Jack" left, I did the same and drove directly to my parents' house. To my surprise, my dad's old girlfriend and her family from Melbourne, Australia had arrived and taken over the house.

My dad had good taste. Marge was beautiful and her husband, Rudy was much older than she. He had been knighted by the Queen of England for donating money to different charities, which made him "Sir Rudy." Supposedly they were super rich. Rudy had forty machine shops and other buildings he was renting out. He had gone to Australia with nothing in his pockets and ended up a multi-millionaire. However, he was very cheap and refused to spend his money on a hotel room for his family.

Their daughter, Susie was my age, Tommy, his first son was two years younger and the other son, Tony, was twelve.

My parents' home had three bedrooms. My sister was living there, so Rudy's daughter stayed with her, the two boys slept on the sofa bed in the living room, and my parents' slept in their bedroom. I ended up sleeping on the floor of the hallway for the few nights I stayed there, but that was enough for me.

Rudy was a multi-millionaire, but refused to spend any money. My parents footed the bill for everything, including their dinners at expensive dining places.

During my visit, Rudy would wake up in the middle of the night, walk around me, and go right to the refrigerator to find something to eat. Even when his kids wanted him to have pizzas delivered to the house, he refused because it "cost too much."

I couldn't believe this guy. Even his wife bitched at him for being such a cheapskate.

One other thing transpired while I was visiting. Tommy had let a couple of people, whom he thought were my friends, into the house when I wasn't there and they had carted away four of my beautiful handmade Afghan carpets that I had rolled up in the bedroom where I used to sleep. They had also taken other expensive and beautiful items that I had brought back with me from my travels. I was really pissed over that. When I called the police, they could do nothing because Tommy couldn't identify the robbers.

I called some of my friends to see if they had heard anything or knew the persons who had stolen my items, but it was no use. I figured it was my old girlfriend, Carol, whose way I had paid to come to Afghanistan. I guessed that she had sent her younger brother to steal the stuff, but I could never prove it. I just gave up and I ended up losing many a friend because of this problem.

After that, I was happy I had moved to Belleville and gotten away from Westland. I figured when the hashish came in, I could return to Asia and buy the country if I wanted. I figured to make between 8 to 12 million on the deal.

THE AGE OF AQUARIUS II

I left my parents' house after three days and returned to the boarding house in Belleville. After unlocking the door to my room, I noticed a couple of telegrams from Amsterdam. They were from Rolf telling me it was a "go" and that the ships would be leaving within two weeks. They would get to America, off the coast of New York, if everything went as planned.

The ships would leave Amsterdam, refuel when they reached Greenland, and head for America. They would give me a certain latitude and longitude; and once there, they would anchor and wait for our boats to unload the illegal contraband.

I couldn't wait. I phoned the few friends who were involved in this operation and told them to get their money together. I also phoned my Uncle Pete concerning certain details relating to the deal, but he refused to speak about it over the phone. He ordered me to meet him at his house the following morning.

I was so anxious and hyped about this deal that I couldn't sleep. I tossed and turned all night long, until about 7 a.m..

After washing up, I went downstairs to the kitchen where the coffee was brewing and had a hot cup. That really woke me up because I hardly ever drank coffee. Usually it was orange juice or hot chicken broth.

A few hours later, I had arrived at my destination.

After parking my car across the street directly in front of Pete's home (his long driveway was full of Caddy's), I ran to the house, jumped the steps two at a time, and rang the doorbell. Once again, my Aunt Helen opened the door, this time with her winter coat on.

"Hello, dear," she said, "Pete's in the living room. I'm on my way to visit your Aunt Virginia. Shut the door behind you." She left in a hurry in the cold morning breeze, driving away in Pete's brand new white Cadillac. She was a nice and beautiful woman, a few inches shorter than Pete, who was about 5'7" but built like Sammy "the bull" Gravano.

When you looked at Pete, with his beady, brown eyes, you knew he wasn't the kind of guy to mess with. I wondered how such a nice lady could have gotten mixed up with him and his crowd. Don't get me wrong; Pete was a nice guy if you were his friend or relative, but if you crossed him, you wouldn't do it again because you'd either end up in the hospital using a walker for the rest of your life, or, if you were lucky, you wouldn't feel a thing, other than a bullet in the back of the head. Thank God I was his friend and relative, although that wouldn't matter if I screwed up, which I hoped I never would.

As soon as I shut the front door, I was met by Sal, who directed me to Pete.

"Have a seat," Pete said from his seat on the living room sofa. "So what's on your mind? What do you want to speak with me about?"

He added, "And from here on out, never—and I mean NEVER—talk about our deal over the phone. The Feds are listening in on all my conversations; the fucking rats. They got no respect for another man's home. They're all pigs! So, let's hear what you got to say…that's so fucking important."

I sat in a chair directly in front of Pete and Sal sat next to him. Louie evidently was a no-show. He still must have been mending his wounds or he would have been at the meeting.

I reached into my coat pocket and pulled out the telegrams I had received from Rolf. I was about to show them to Pete when there was a knock at the door. Immediately, Sal jumped up from his seat to answer it. I thought Louie was the person knocking, but to my surprise, it was Mr. Giacalone. We all stood up when he came into the room. Sal helped him off with his coat and hat and set them down neatly over the back of a reclining chair.

Mr. Giacalone rubbed his hands to warm them. We all moved into the dining room and sat at the dining room table, sitting in the same seats as before.

"So what the fuck is up?" Giacalone asked, with a cold stare in his eyes. "What the fuck's so important that you get me out here so early in the morning?"

I opened my mouth to speak, but Pete gestured that I was to say nothing until told to do so. I kept my mouth shut and let Pete do the talking. "Give me the telegrams." he ordered. I did, nervously. Pete then read the three telegrams from Rolf and handed them to Giacalone to read.

After Giacalone had read them, he folded his hands and didn't say a word for a good minute. You could see him thinking, thinking about what he was about to say.

I nervously waited to hear his words, but what I really wanted to do was take a piss. However, now I would have pissed in my pants, rather than interrupt Giacalone's thoughts.

I had gotten myself into the gangster life. But hell, I was just a young hippie wanting to get high on the best hash I could buy…or morphine. I could have bought and sold heroin that Pete had in large quantities; at one time, he had shown me a bag of it. I figured it was at least a kilo of pure heroin, like the stuff Daniel was sending me, but my stupidity ended that deal.

I had the people to sell it to, but they all carried guns….and used them. I didn't want any part of it; just like I didn't want any part in dealing with the Mob, but now it was too late. I was far too deep into a place I didn't want to be in, but what could I do? I was now an associate of the Detroit Mafia and Pete was my main connection. If he told me to sell his heroin or cocaine or whatever drug, I'd be a fool to turn him down. I knew if I did that, I wouldn't have too long to live on this earth. For now, though, Pete hadn't asked or told me to sell anything for him. I was the one that wanted him to sell my illegal drugs.

All I was thinking at that time was that I wished I could have snapped my fingers and "whoosh" I'd be in the "Land of Oz." My magical thoughts, however, were interrupted when

Giacalone began to speak. Goosebumps ran down my spine when he looked directly into my eyes.

"Fuck the latitude and longitude," he said. "I've spoken with Don Gambino and underbosses, Neil Delecroche and Paul Castellano. You wire your connection in Amsterdam and tell him to bring his ships directly into New York City Harbor and dock them at pier 10, right behind the cargo containers. We'll unload the cargo there and take the hashish to a Gambino owned warehouse, then we'll distribute it across the country."

That would be much easier than to have fifty small boats all leaving their marinas at the same time, which might alert the authorities that something unusual was happening and increase the risk of us ending up in jail. No one faced the chance of jail time while unloading the contraband from the ships onto boats, since the Gambino family had control of NYC docks. The Harbor Master, Harbor Patrol, and even Customs were in their pockets, and that included the NYC detectives and police who made sure that nobody fucked with the cargo.

All five New York families did this on a daily basis. There was one small problem, however. They didn't have the Coast Guard on their payroll. Even so, that didn't seem to bother the "Big Boys," because the Coast Guard could be outmaneuvered and misdirected.

So I didn't protest. What good would it have done if I had? They certainly had planned it better than I had. Hell, they even had the mayor on their payroll. All I had to do now was to wire Rolf with this new information. I was sure he wouldn't object and would go for the deal. It made sense; less hassles all around.

Pete's truck drivers (all Teamsters) would load the product into their trucks and then drive six-hundred miles to one of Pete's warehouses in Detroit, where it would be unloaded. From there, I could take it by cars, vans, or small delivery trucks and distribute it to my drug connections. That, however, would entail many trips to and fro.

THE AGE OF AQUARIUS II

Pete would see to it that all went according to plan. He also had the Detroit police and many politicians on his payroll. Therefore, even with all the traffic going in and out of the warehouse, there would be no problems. That is, except for mine; in the form of distributing nearly one hundred tons of Lebanese hashish, less the twenty percent the Mob was getting: This meant I had to unload eighty tons.

Well, time was of the essence and Giacalone had other important matters to take care of, so our little sit-down wound down.

We all shook hands as we said our goodbyes. Pete walked me to the front door afterward. "You wire Rolf about the change in plans. I'll be contacting you in a few days about a small job," he said.

It turned out I was to drive him and Sal to Cleveland, Ohio to meet with the boss and underbosses of the Mel Field Road Mob.

After that meeting, I learned the MFL Mob was having trouble with an Irishman named Danny Green. He was stealing the Mob's trucks after they had hijacked them.

In addition, many of the Mob's crew members were suddenly getting busted for one reason or another. They believed that Danny Green was an informant for the FBI and they wanted him dead—NOW!

A number of tries to take him out had failed. Now they called in Pete's crew from Detroit. Actually, the underboss from Cleveland had a sit-down with Tony Giacalone and he, in turn, gave the job to his #1 crew. Pete and his henchmen were called on to end the Mel Field Road Mob's problem.

It was a fact that the two Mafia Mobs had been connected since the early 1920's and were part of the Purple Gang, smuggling many types of liquor from Windsor, Canada to Detroit and Cleveland. However, with prohibition over for more than 45 years, drugs were now the big money maker, taking the place of alcohol. Instead of liquid it was powders—cocaine and heroin, which came through Montreal and New

York harbors, to then be shipped by tanker trucks or hidden in the trunks of the new cars on two tier trailers driven by Teamsters' truck drivers. They were taken to the Teamsters' warewarehouses to be distributed to Mobs all around the country, but mostly to Detroit and Cleveland, where the drugs were cut from 89-99% purity to 2-10% purity.

For instance, Pete would receive 30 kilos of 99% white heroin from Thailand, have his crews cut it into 150-200 kilos or more of 2-10% heroin and then distribute it throughout the country to many of the Mafia families. Pete and his bosses made a fortune from the white powders.

How could one turn down such a lucrative business? And that's what Pete and his crew saw it as—a business. Even though it destroyed families, and sometimes their own, the money being made was too hard to overlook.

The #1 rule in Pete's crew and others in the Detroit Mob: never use drugs. If you did, they had an easy solution: You got WHACKED! Whether it be your brother, yourself or anyone else in La Cosa Nostra, it didn't matter. You got WHACKED!

4

CHAPTER

Plans have changed

As the door closed behind me, I stood on the porch for a few seconds, breathing in the cool, crisp air. I lit a cigarette as I walked down the steps to my car.

I drove back to my boarding house. My conscience wouldn't allow me to "forget." I thought to myself over and over again, *What the hell have I gotten myself into?* I had thought those same words the first time I asked my Uncle Pete to help me with my "problem."

I wasn't just my Uncle's driver any longer. I was now "one of them" and had no choice in the matter. I was "under their thumb," which meant they could put the "screws" to me at any time, for any reason. If I refused—Whack, murder time. I would end up "food for the fishes or for the "worms." It didn't matter. You ended up dead. So, through my stupidity, I was now my Uncle Pete's "Boy," to use as he pleased.

The thought of murder sickened me, because I now knew it was now just a matter of time until they would tell me it was my turn to "whack" one of their own or an enemy. I had a feeling the trip to Cleveland was the reason I was asked to go along. I would not be just driving them there; it was a trip for me to make my "bones"—to murder this guy, Danny Green, or at the very least, to help with the murder. That just wasn't my bag. I was a "hippie," a "lover of peace," not some guy without a conscience who could kill without any regrets. But then again, if my Uncle ordered me to kill the guy, to show the others that I had the "balls" to commit murder for the "good" of the Family, then that would show them that I could be trusted—to do as ordered with no repercussions.

This is why I kept telling myself, *"What the fuck have I gotten myself into?"* Was the money worth the sickening feeling I would have to live with, day and night, trying not to think about the people I had killed for the "Family?" I didn't think so, but there was no going back now. I was in it up to my knees; all because I wanted to do this deal with Rolf. I thought I could handle it myself, but oh how wrong I was.

One thing I did have going for me, if an order to murder ever transpired—I had plenty of drugs to take that would help me sleep, while taking my mind off the ruthless being I might become.

I now knew I could never get away from this new family who had adopted me. I considered for a few seconds to get out now and return to Afghanistan: the country that I had never wanted to leave, but at this point in time, I couldn't. No money...and I had to get this operation completed and get the Mob the money and dope that they expected for doing me this "favor."

Now I had to wire Rolf about the change in plans—to bring his three ships to the docks of New York City Harbor instead of staying outside the twelve mile limit and unloading the hundred tons of hash onto smaller vessels.

If things went as planned, the operation would go much faster and safer, especially if the New York Mob had Customs and the Harbor Master in their pocket. We would be unloading the contraband onto forty-foot tractor trailers, drive the big rigs to a Gambino warehouse for safekeeping, and then driving them to Detroit to one of the warehouses that was actually owned by the Teamsters Union.

Once inside my bedroom at the boarding house, I took my "works" out of a small bag hidden in my groin area. I always carried this with me, along with three half-grain morphine tablets that I had purchased from a guy who was a night janitor and worked at a pharmacy that had been in business for nearly 100 years. I purchased every tablet of morphine he could steal, which was 200. I quickly did my "fix" and once my rush had subsided, I got out my hash pipe and took a few tokes of some Affy hashish. The high took my mind off my "problems" and allowed me to fall to sleep.

Now I had morphine, but not much hash left. I had sold most of it to my close friends and only had a few ounces left. Soon, though, I would have more hashish than I knew what to do with.

The next morning, I wired Rolf with new instructions for unloading the contraband. I received his answer two days later.

Rolf, having done business with the New York Mob years before, had agreed to the new orders. However, one ship had engine problems and was not completely ready to get underway. It seemed that work on one of the two Diesel engines would take approximately another week before it would be seaworthy. Lots of money was at stake and Rolf didn't want to take any chances until it was 100% ready for the open seas.

Rolf was considering placing less hashish on this particular vessel, just in case something unexpected happened while sailing the Atlantic Ocean. He figured if something should happen to that ship, the Coast Guard would rescue it and most likely find the contraband, even though it was well hidden in the tires for giant hydraulic Hi-Los.

Hash was shipped many times using this way of hiding it and it worked without any problems. Rolf believed it would work this time also, as long as there weren't any outrageous storms or Hurricanes and especially any problems that the ships' mechanics couldn't handle.

I phoned Pete and told him, "It's a Go." He then relayed the message to Giacalone, who in turn relayed the message to the "Families" in New York.

Rolf figured everything would be ready within a week or two, depending on how well the mechanics inspected each ship before leaving for New York.

Pete called me over to his place a few days later and gave me the low-down about the trip to Cleveland. I was to drive his Caddy. Three of us would be going: Pete, Sal and me. Louie was still under the weather after the shooting, which had infected his shoulder. I assumed I was taking his place.

No matter, I wasn't looking forward to the visit. This deal wasn't going as I had planned and had gotten me deeper and deeper into a "black hole." Already, I had been involved with one shooting and now I assumed there was about to be another. *But what could I do? Not a damn thing.* At least until Rolf's deal was finished. And then I wasn't sure about that.

If the Mob decided to keep all of the contraband, what could I do? They take the hashish, make the money, whack me and throw me into the dirty Hudson River where many a body lay.

I did not make a good gangster....and didn't want to be. But there I was—a gangster.

Once the sit-down with Pete was over, I was told to be ready to move out within two days. We would be gone—that is, if everything went as planned—for about two days. It would take me about three to five hours, depending on traffic, to get to the safe house, where we were to stay.

There were five members of the MFR crew at the house when we arrived, including the underboss, Jack Licavoli. I was told this underboss went back to the days of the "Purple Gang" and was one mean SOB.

"You!" roared Licavoli, pointing at me. "Sit in the kitchen!" When I didn't move fast enough, Licavoli grabbed me by my coat and threw me across the room. "Get your ass in gear when I tell you to do something."

Pete told him, "Take it easy on the kid; he's my nephew."

Licavoli didn't seem to care. He said to Pete, "The kid should do as he's told."

Hell, I didn't even have time to stand up from the couch before being thrown across the room, where most of his crew was playing cards. They asked me a few unimportant questions, which I refused to answer, and within half-an-hour, the MFR crew had left the house.

Pete later asked how I was. "Don't let that asshole fuck with your mind. He's an animal." He rubbed my head, as if I was a ten year old kid, and then we went out to eat at an Italian restaurant.

Afterwards I was told what was going to be happening. I already had an idea. Luckily, I was to stay at the safe house and keep an eye open for the cops and any of the MFR crew. Pete, Sal, and two of the MFR crew were to do the job of whacking this Irishman. Evidently, it was a rather touchy situation because this guy, Danny, had the backing of some Italian Mob and Teamster member named John Nardi. His crew would not be happy about the hit, but the MFR crew didn't care.

During the meeting, Al, one of the MFR crew members, had told Pete, "If Nardi or any of his crew get in the way, whack them too."

However, Nardi was a made man and Pete would have to get the Ok from the five families before whacking him.

Licavoli told Pete, "It's already taken care of."

Pete, however, didn't believe him and called Giacalone to make sure that what Licavoli said was true. Evidently, it was. Everyone in the Detroit and Cleveland mobs believed Green to be a "Rat." And they surmised if Green was a "Rat," so was Nardi. At least, that's how it was explained to me. So the hit was a "go."

The following night was the designated time to rid the world of the "Irish Rat." If Nardi gave the MFR crew any shit, he was to become an "expendable asset" also.

I thanked Pete for "keeping me out of the hit," but was dumbfounded when he told me, "It wasn't my doing. It was Licavoli's idea."

According to Pete, Licavoli wanted his guys to go along and help out rather than me. So this guy who threw me across the room into the kitchen was actually my "savior."

I was to be the "gopher."

I drove Pete and Sal to an Italian restaurant a few blocks from the safe house, where we ate salad, Spaghetti, Ravioli, Garlic bread, and drank two bottles of a sweet red wine. However, because of the drugs I had consumed, I didn't drink the wine and had water instead.

When supper was over, Pete instructed me to stop at a liquor store to buy a couple of bottles of Vodka, Whiskey, and some snacks to eat at a later time, and the local newspaper. He also had me stop at an Army and Navy store to buy some English and Irish miniature flags. I didn't question him about this, but did as ordered. I figured that it had something to do with the Danny Green problem. I surmised one of the guys would place them in Green's hands to throw the cops off on the hit, letting them think that the British Intelligence had killed him or his own IRA people. No one told me this, but I was sure Pete wasn't taking them home as tourist gifts.

When we returned to the safe house, Pete took the newspaper out of the bag and began reading it as he munched on a Kit Kat candy bar.

On the front page of the local paper was a picture of John Scalish, Cleveland's Mob boss, along with an article about his poor health and heart problems. Coincidently, on the lower left hand corner of the same page, was a picture and article of MFR crew's nemesis, Danny Green, who was explaining to the journalist that if "anyone came after him, the British Intelligence, Blacks or the Italian Mob, he could take care of himself." He made it sound as though he was an IRA member, not a member of an Irish Mob, and was against the British Government.

After Pete got through reading the article, he told Sal that they would make the hit look as though the British Government's security people had done it, using the British Flags I had bought at the Army & Navy store. They'd place them into Green's hands to make it look as though the British killed another member of the terrorist group, the IRA.

I had surmised correctly.

That morning, we went to a small restaurant about two miles away from the safe house and ate a hefty breakfast. Afterwards, Pete made a telephone call to the guys who were to help in the mission and told them to keep a tail on Green so we could hit him in front of an Irish Bar where he was known to sit outside, even though it was colder than hell, drinking coffee laced with Irish whiskey. His security team either sat with him or sat in the bar when the weather was too cold. Green wouldn't shy away from his enemies but egged them on to "come and get him." The other place he hung out was just around the corner from the bar—his apartment building with a large parking lot and lots of trees and shrubs surrounding it. It gave Pete and the guys all the protection they needed against being seen.

I couldn't believe the way Green showed himself to the world, with Irish Flags flowing in the wind above his head, always dressed in green. Even his Caddy was green and taunted anyone who had the "balls" to try their luck to kill him.

Just around dusk, Pete received the phone call that he had been waiting for. Green was walking from the bar to his apartment building, with approximately six or more bodyguards surrounding him.

Pete's crew was just a few minutes away. They hurriedly checked their weapons to make sure they were loaded and told me to keep an eye on the safe house and television. They left in a wink of an eye, with Sal carrying the flags.

I peeked out the front window. I could see Sal sitting behind the steering wheel. Just as they were leaving, two of the MFR crew members loaded into Pete's Caddy and Sal peeled out of the driveway as fast as the car could go, to make the hit before Green entered the apartment building.

Once Pete and his crew were gone, I grabbed a bag of chips, soda pop, and turned the television to the news station, before resting on the sofa.

I was nervous as hell. Sitting in an old, dilapidated building that smelled of mildew, cigarettes and alcohol, I was now part of a conspiracy—a conspiracy to commit murder.

If Pete and the guys did their job correctly, the TV media would be at the murder scene within minutes because Green was a big Media figure.

About 45 minutes after leaving the safe house, Pete and Sal returned—out of breath, pissed off, cursing loudly, and in a very bad mood. I kept my mouth shut, which was a smart move because eventually I learned the news that the hit went terribly wrong. Sal was wounded in his right arm, but just a scratch. He was lucky; the bullet creased the outside of his bicep, while one of the MFR crew was killed. Danny Green had shot three guys, killing one and wounding two of the "hit men."

Everyone got away clean, except the guy who was killed. Pete stated that Green had "balls of steel." When the shooting began, Green was alone, but he always carried a gun. When shot at, he stood his ground and returned fire. Evidently he was an excellent shot.

"Those MFR scumbags ran like chickens with their heads cut off," Pete cursed. "We stood our ground, but there were too many cars for Green to hide behind. I couldn't fire an accurate shot. I must have fired thirty shots, but not one bullet hit Green."

The media showed up to interview the target, and Green seemed to be the "hero" of the day. All the Irish ethnic groups came out, surrounding him like it was Saint Patrick's Day and he was Saint Patrick.

The TV news crews showed up and interviewed Green while the cops were sealing off the crime scene and canvassing the area. The cops found a number of rounds from the guns that were used.

Every channel showed the same people, out celebrating their hero and shoving each other out of the way to get an interview with the Mob's nemesis. Danny Green had a smile a mile long and told the news media that if anyone else tried to kill him, they'd get the same as he gave the dead guy.

We waited until the following morning before leaving the state and I drove back to Michigan in record time, just as I had returning from New Jersey. At least this time I didn't get shot at and have bullets whistling around my head.

5

CHAPTER

Returning home

To say the least, the ride returning to Michigan was an ordeal. Sal, a big, heavy-set, six-foot-plus gangster was whining because of a flesh wound, like a two year old baby who had lost his pacifier. *Give me a break*, I thought to myself. And this guy is a "Gangster!" What a laugh.

    Not only did I have to put up with Sal's whining, I had to listen to Pete's excuses that he planned to tell Giacalone about why they couldn't do the job they were sent to do. Both were taking their problems out on me.

    Pete yelled to me, "Slow Down! You're driving too fast! You're gonna have the police on our tail if you keep driving the way you are!" This kept up constantly during the three hour drive.

    It was driving me crazy. I wanted to stop the car and say to Pete, "Fuck it! You Drive!" And to Sal, "Quit Whining like a little baby. You make me sick!"

    I pulled into Pete's driveway; Just then, we noticed that Giacalone's car was also in the driveway. All that came out of

Pete's mouth was, "Oh, FUCK!" He seemed to be a little upset and very worried.

Before getting out of the car, he checked his fifteen round clip to make sure that his gun was fully loaded. He placed the weapon into the back of his pants; the tightness of his belt kept it in place. He zipped up his coat, and we stepped out of the vehicle.

Walking up the steps to his house, I noticed that Pete seemed very nervous; his hands were shaking. Before opening up the door, he placed his right hand on the pistol, breathed deeply. Just as he put his key into the lock, the door opened. Giacalone was standing in the foyer, with a look that made my knees weak

He stepped back as Pete, Sal and I walked into the house. Then Giacalone said, "What the fuck happened back there?"

I surmised that he meant Cleveland. You could see he was rather upset, to say the least. At that point in time, I wanted to be a thousand miles away, but unfortunately I was part of the crew that "FUCKED UP!"

Pete just stood his ground and said, "You don't want to know."

"Like hell I don't." snapped Giacalone, as he turned and walked into the living room. The three of us followed him.

Giacalone sat down on the couch and then bellowed, "I'll ask you one more time, Pete, what the fuck happened?"

Before answering, Pete took off his coat, took his gun out of the back of his pants, placed it into his coat pocket, and began giving Giacalone excuses.

Pete's wife came into the room. "Anyone want coffee?" she asked.

"Get the fuck outta here!" snapped Giacalone in his deep thuggish voice.

He talked like that to Pete's wife and Pete said nothing. I thought to myself, *Hell, Pete's a made man, a capo, and takes that shit from Giacalone.* I knew Pete wasn't afraid of him, so I figured that he must have had a good reason for not doing anything about it. If he whacked the guy for running his mouth about his wife, without the Ok of the commission, I surmised that he and his whole family would get whacked, cut up into little pieces, and used as fish bait.

Then Pete spoke up. "We fucked up. It's as simple as that."

"You Goddamned right you fucked up," Giacalone bellowed. "You're lucky I don't have your entire crew whacked. The Cleveland boys are all over my ass and now I have to explain this to the commission."

Pete replied, "What can I tell you? This guy Danny Green was waiting for us. I figure he was tipped off. Either one of the Cleveland guys tipped him…or, like we thought, he's got an in with the cops or FBI. That's what I figure."

"And what do you figure, Sal?" asked Giacalone, giving him a dirty look, He then added, "Forget it. You ain't got the fucking brains to give me an opinion."

"Mr. Giacalone," Sal retorted, "I did my best. Fuck, I got hit trying to kill that Irish bastard. And one of the two Cleveland guys got whacked by Green." He took off his coat and showed Giacalone his flesh wound.

"Shit. You got hit? The way you drink, Sal, it looks like you got drunk and fell and scraped your arm on the edge of a coffee table," said Giacalone.

Sal just looked at Giacalone with disgust and shrugged his shoulders.

"Look Boss, you can bitch at me all you want," Pete told Giacalone. "I'm responsible for the hit not going as planned, but Sal was nearly killed trying to kill that crazy Irishman. If I was you, I'd ask the Cleveland Boss who tipped off Green. I'm telling you, this guy knew we were coming. It don't take a brain scientist to know that, if you'd seen what went down."

Giacalone held up his right hand to stop Pete from saying anything more. He was pissed because his crew was the best at whacking people, only behind the Roy DeMayo crew of the Gambino Family who killed people just to kill, even their own.

Giacalone stood up and put on his coat. "We'll take this up at a later time," he said to Pete. "I have business elsewhere and some explaining to do concerning this Green thing."

He said goodbye to Pete's wife and walked to the front door to leave. He saw Pete's car behind his, making it impossible for him to leave. He turned to say something about this problem, but I acted immediately.

I had the keys to Pete's car in my pants pocket, so I stood up and ran out of the house to move Pete's car so Giacalone could leave. I walked back into the house as Giacalone was backing out of the driveway.

As I shut the door, I noticed that Pete's wife had cleaned Sal's wound and bandaged it. Sal thanked her, grabbed his coat, and put it over his shoulders.

We had picked him up at his house before leaving for Cleveland so Pete ordered me to drive Sal home and return immediately.

As I drove Sal home (he was still living with his mother), he kept bitching about Giacalone giving him a hard time over something that wasn't his fault. Actually, the way Sal explained things, one of the Cleveland guys jumped in front of his gun as he fired and it was he who killed the Cleveland guy. Had the guy not jumped in front of Sal's gun, I surmised to get credit for killing the Irishman, he probably would still be alive today and Sal and the other guy wouldn't have been hit by Green and Green probably would have been shot and killed by Sal. Sal would have dropped the flags on the dead body; or placed them in Green's hands.

Whatever happened, the hit had been poorly coordinated. Pete should have never allowed those Cleveland guys to be part of it. I supposed, although, he had no other choice in the matter. Giacalone had ordered him to do the hit as a favor to the MFR hierarchy and they, in turn, had ordered Pete to take a couple of their guys with him and Sal. According to both Pete and Sal, the Cleveland guys were a bunch of simpletons who didn't know what their right and left hands were doing. They were the downfall of this exhibition in Mob killing. Their soldiers were stupid, didn't graduate High School, let alone go to College, maybe except to the college of "hard knocks" and street thuggery.

The year was nearing an end; 1975 was just around the corner and Nixon had resigned as President for being an "idiot."

I was sure "someone" was going down for the drastic mistake made in Cleveland. And you can bet your bottom dollar it wasn't going to be Giacalone, once he talked to his superiors on the New York Committee—the hierarchy of the five families. I was sure it would be up to them to decide who would live and die over this "Fuck up."

I would bet my life on it that the MFR crew was on the phones talking to the members of the five families, or possibly sending one of their underbosses to New York, wanting more blood for the blood spilt when one of their soldiers was killed.

Pete had planned the hit, so my bet was on him taking the fall. This is what I thought as I drove Sal to his house, walking him to the door, and then returning to Pete's house for orders. Then I thought, *shit, I was a newcomer and just the person to blame all this confusion on.* However, I came back to Earth when I figured they wouldn't do anything to me. I had a big deal in the works that would make some decent money for some, if not all, of the five families. I was an asset to them, not an excuse. Realizing this seemed to calm my nervous body by the time I drove into Pete's driveway. I sat in the car for a few minutes, trying to figure out any answers to the questions that might come my way. Taking a deep breath, I slowly got out of the car, quietly shut the door behind me and walked up the eight long steps that seemed like a thousand. I knocked on the door and Helen opened it. She told me to go into the living room, where Pete was waiting for me.

She had a nervous tone in her voice, which didn't give me much hope. It took everything inside of me to muscle up enough strength just to get my legs moving in that direction. I took it one step at a time, the thirty steps from the foyer to the living room also took forever. Pete was sitting on the couch, sipping a very small cup of Italian coffee; Espresso, I think it was called.

Pete saw me come in and motioned for me to take a seat across from him. It was a plush chair, so plush in fact, that I sank nearly a foot, before my knees came up to my chin. The room was silent for a good two minutes while Pete drank his Espresso. He finally put the cup on the table in front of him. I tried to speak, but nothing came out of my mouth. Pete beat me to it anyway.

"Hey, kid," Pete said in a gentle tone—if gangsters have a gentle tone. But I think he was talking as my Uncle, not as an employer. "Don't let any of this worry you. This is family business. Not yours. Whatever happens…to me, Sal, or whomever, don't let it worry you. Someone from this family will tell you what to do. And right now, I want you to go home, get some rest. Then wire this guy, Rolf, and tell him that we are ready on our end. If, for some reason, you don't hear from me, which I'm sure won't happen, you see Sal. He knows what needs to be done. He's my number one GOOMBA. So, take off home and I'll call you tomorrow, just to let you know everything is all right. And if you hear from your friend in Amsterdam, tell him to get his shit together because Christmas is just around the corner. But that may not be so bad. The Coast Guard will be patrolling for accidents and lost boats and I'm sure we'll put out a distress call or two. So, now, go home and rest up and everything will come out smelling of roses." With that said, he stood up, gave me a hug, and kissed me on both cheeks.

"I was always jealous of your father," he said. The revelation shocked me. "If I'd ever had a son, I'd want him to be just like you. In a few years, we would have opened the books, and you could have become a made man like me. Who knows? OK. Go home, get some rest, and then wire your friend to get this thing of his under way."

I then turned and walked to the front door. My Aunt Helen let me out after I kissed her on the cheek, then I told her that I'd say "Hello" to my mom for her. "Take care, Aunt Helen."

I walked out the door and into my car. It took a good three long starts before my car started, but she never failed me, my one and a half year old, 1973 Vega Hatchback with a 3-speed on the floor. It was a nice car and my only transportation. However, I needed to get my brakes fixed, and soon, with more than fifty-thousand miles on the drums and rotors. Money was my only drawback and in short supply.

Pete paid me nothing for driving to and fro to Cleveland, New York, and New Jersey. I guess he figured he was doing me a favor and I owed him, rather than vice versa. However, I didn't see it that way. This score from the hash deal would make all of us hundreds of millions of dollars—depending on the price we sold it for. Not quite as much money as they made from heroin. After cutting it with quinine or other ingredients, one kilo of pure smack would make more than 100 kilos, which sold at $100,000 per. One kilo of hashish sold from five-hundred to one-thousand dollars.

Even though we wouldn't make as much profit as the heroin, if caught with hash, the jail time was only a year or so. Getting busted with just one kilo of heroin was life plus one thousand years.

Rolf, hopefully soon, would be sending at least one hundred tons of "primo" hash, which equaled two hundred thousand pounds. Minus the twenty percent the Gambino Family cut would be, that left 160,000 pounds. And then you had to count what the Zerilli Family cut would be; certainly not twenty percent. I would have to talk with Pete and Giacalone concerning this.

If the Detroit Family received the same as the New York and New Jersey Families were getting, that would leave Rolf and I with 160,000 pounds of primo Lebanese Hashish. Cut in half, that would leave Rolf and I around 80,000 lbs each. If sold at one thousand dollars per pound, that would leave us each with a profit of 80 million. Cut that profit in half, if sold for five hundred dollars per pound— that would leave each of us with a profit of 40 million.

If the trip went as planned I would make it to the "Big Time." Both Pete and the New York and New Jersey Families would be proud of me. I would be considered a "Big Earner," which would be a good...or bad thing.

It would be considered a bad thing if the Families expected that kind of money from me and Rolf yearly.

Rolf was getting old and wanted to retire from the business. I then would ask him for his connections, hoping that he would turn me onto them if and when retirement was a done deal. However, that was a dream, not reality. Then again, I didn't know if I could handle all the stress that came with the business. I mean, I was used to dealing with the hash growers, especially from what I had learned from the years of dealing with the Mujahedeen of Afghanistan.

The other part of the business was the headaches from dealing with the Mob and the people in my distribution network. For instance, my people could make $2,000.00 from a selling a pound of excellent quality hashish, only there was a major problem. We needed to sell the one-hundred ton shipment as quickly as possible so Rolf could get his money, in case he wanted to buy another shipment from Baalbek. He probably needed to update his transportation for carrying the next load of contraband much more easily from Lebanon to America.

I also needed to update my transportation to load the hashish, which wasn't a problem. Unloading the stuff to four major cities was my main concern. I would most likely pick out a few trustworthy, close friends who had basements, to whom I could transport maybe one or two-hundred pounds each to use as launching pads.

I would also use the pollen or powder in the sacks and make hash that would look like Affy and taste and smoke just like it. I would only use the best sack hash for this process. I had done this in my earlier career as a hash dealer.

If Rolf sent some excellent green sack hash, which looked and smelled just like Afghani, I would use the Afghani way of making hash, press it into Affy, and sell it for the Affy prices, not the Lebanese prices. This would double or triple my profits and the people would actually think they were smoking Affy.

Most of the sack hash I used before to press into what looked like Affy had come from plants that were at least twenty-five feet tall, had two feet stalks and foot long, eight inch round colas (buds) or bigger. This stuff was very similar to what I used to press into Affy and this particular Lebanese was as good as any Affy that I had gotten from the Balkh Province, which was #1 pollen and cost five times more than the average Affy pollen.

The following morning, after eating breakfast, I went to my local supermarket and sent Rolf a wire concerning the change in plans. I was sure he would go for it. If not, I figured the Mob would have one or two of their soldiers in Amsterdam change his mind. If not, he would end up dead. That was a "given." Then the Mob would run the whole operation.

However, before killing Rolf, most likely the hit men would torture him to get the information needed concerning the ships and dope.

Evidently, Rolf also figured what would happen to him if he didn't go along with the change in plans and wired me a "Go," which was the code word for "ship." If only one ship left port, he would wire the word "Go." If all three ships left port he would wire "Go" three times, which meant all three ships had left port and were heading for America and New York Harbor

Three days later, I received the wire I had been waiting for. It stated "Go, Go, Go," December 4th. However, it also stated, "engine problem still exists, will be first to go, others will follow.

As soon as I got the wire from Rolf, I phoned Pete. However, he wouldn't discuss business over the phone, so I had to drive to his home and fill him in on the project.

Once inside his house, I showed him the wire I had received from Rolf. A big smile crossed his face. I could see dollar signs in his eyes.

In turn, he contacted Giacalone, and Giacalone contacted the Gambino's most powerful underboss, Neil Delecroche, and gave him the news.

Pete and I figured that, if all went well, the ships wouldn't reach New York Harbor for at least two weeks or longer.

I hoped I would be able to begin distributing and selling the hash to my connections a week or so before Christmas. That would definitely make a "Merry Christmas" for many people and keep me in good with Pete and his crew, which would make Pete a well-known name with the Gambino Mob. Now all we could do was wait for the next wire from Rolf.

Pete and I kept in contact daily and at times I would be his gopher and pick up money from his numbers racket, which made him a pretty good profit weekly. Many times, he had me count the money on his dining room table to make sure none of his people had ripped him off. One week, I counted more than seventy thousand dollars. After giving twenty-percent to Giacalone, he usually made approximately fifty thousand or more, just from that one racket. I knew of a half-dozen other rackets that were just as profitable.

The following morning, after counting out the money for Pete, I received a wire from Rolf stating, "Go, Go, Go; left

Greenland. Be home soon," which meant that all three ships were refueled and heading for New York Harbor.

The dockworkers were ready to unload the contraband and the trucks were also ready and waiting for the word.

Two days later, I was driving Pete, Sal, and Louie in Pete's big Caddy, heading to Mulberry Street in Queens, where a safe house was ready for its guests to overlook the unloading of the precious cargo.

It was already the 12th of December and we figured two to four days and the ships would arrive. We calculated, at twenty knots, twenty-four hours per day, the ships would cover well over five-hundred miles a day.

Pete ordered me to wire Rolf to make sure all was well. The reply wasn't what we expected.

The ship with the engine problem was running only on one diesel, not two. It was fifty miles behind the other two ships.

Those were the last words we heard. From that point on, we were in the dark concerning the ships and contraband.

We spent five days in a small one-bedroom home which housed four of us; Pete, Sal, Louie and me. We had planned on spending only two or three days at the most and, at times, were getting edgy and always complaining about one thing or another. I would quiet the arguing by reminding them about the money we were going to make on this deal if everything went according to plan. So far, however, things weren't going as planned.

Finally, the day had arrived when we received word that one of the ships had entered and docked at New York City Harbor. And it was huge: a smaller version of a cargo container.

Delecroche and Corallo stayed behind and sent Angie Ruggerio, the guy I had met in New Jersey when Pete had the sit-down. He was responsible for the unloading of the contraband and for making sure that none of the dockworkers took any for themselves.

THE AGE OF AQUARIUS II

After the Captain signed in at the Harbor Master's office and Ok'd the shipment, the dockworkers were given the Ok to unload hundreds of giant Hi-Lo tires.

We were expecting thirty-two to thirty-three tons of quality Lebanese hashish, but the final count was twenty-two tons.

When Angie notified Delecroche of this, he was pissed, to say the least, and was ready to have the Captain whacked, including the crew of seven. That was, until the Captain explained the situation on board his ship.

The Captain handed out glasses to Angie, Pete, Sal, Louie and me, and filled them with a fine brand of whiskey. After the Captain consumed his drink in one gulp, he began nervously to explain what had happened to the missing eleven tons of hash and the other two ships.

The Captain cleared his throat, and said, "My boss, Rolf, has fucked this up from the beginning, sending old, unseaworthy and rusty ships for such a big and expensive operation."

He continued. "As soon as the ships left the port of Amsterdam, problems arose. Rough seas and stormy weather began approximately two miles into the trip to Greenland. Ten to twelve feet waves were constant, which made the ships use more fuel than anticipated.

"Each ship had three fifty-five gallon barrels of diesel fuel on board in case of hazardous conditions. The seven men crews were constantly tying things down, some men nearly falling overboard. Even though the barrels of diesel fuel were chained down, the treacherous waves and windy conditions gave my ship constant trouble, breaking loose and spilling all over the deck. We lost more than half of one barrel before it could be chained again to the stern of the ship.

"My ship had constant engine problems. They had been fixed in Amsterdam, but halfway through the voyage to Greenland, one engine continued giving the mechanic problems until it shut down with a plugged valve. We had to run on a single screw (propeller), instead of two, which made it difficult for me to keep the ship on course, let alone to keep up with the other two vessels. We came into the port in Greenland two hours behind the others. The engine was repaired again and we left Greenland eight hours before the others in case engine problems arose. Problems did happen again, approximately two-hundred miles from New York City Harbor.

"Because of the constant engine problems, we took eleven tons of hashish off my ship before we left Greenland and put it onto the best ship out of the three. This is why my ship came into port with only twenty-two tons instead of thirty-three.

"Another of the three ships also had problems with tied down equipment becoming untied, such as fishing nets and other important fishing items that fell overboard and could not be retrieved. Some of the heavy equipment broke free and pinned one of the crew, breaking his arm. It was set by another crew member without pain medication and the man was left in a hospital in Greenland."

The Captain filled his pipe with tobacco, lit it, and again filled our glasses with whiskey. He drank his down and took a few long puffs on his pipe.

However, before the Captain was able to speak again, Pete brought up the subject on the whereabouts of the other two ships.

Pete asked, "Where are the other ships? There are five tractor-trailers, each with forty-foot trailers, ready to carry the contraband. The dock workers are waiting to unload the other two ships and they are very nervous and bored. I'm paying them to just stand around or eat their lunches and I don't like that."

They didn't wait long, though. If all hundred tons had made it into NY Harbor, we'd have needed nearly 40 tractor-trailers. However, we did have enough trucks for the twenty-two ton shipment.

THE AGE OF AQUARIUS II

The Captain continued. "Because weather conditions were so treacherous, two members from two different ships returned to Amsterdam by plane, including the one who had his arm reset; he had his fill of the sea after twenty-two years. In fact, a few other members from each ship were injured, not seriously though, while refueling the engines in forty mph. winds and squalls as they traveled to Greenland. And by the time the three Captains found new crew members for the deserting crew members, the trip was three days late of its scheduled time to reach New York Harbor."

#

When the first ship arrived, everyone was elated. However, when we learned that this was the only ship that would arrive in port, our elation turned into frustration. The frustration then turned into anger when it was found out that the Bonanno family in Montreal would get the largest shipment of the two that had made it into port because, twelve miles from New York City Harbor, the Coast Guard had intercepted the ship that had the extra eleven tons of hashish aboard.

And when it was learned that Corallo had asked the Bonanno Family to make sure the ship came into the port of Montreal safely, all hell broke loose because the Gambino and Lucchese families were to earn an equal portion of the money made from the contraband. To save face and to avoid a war between the Gambino, Lucchese, and Bonanno families, they agreed to share the profits equally.

Pete was not happy over this, nor was Giacalone, and neither was I, due to the fact that I was completely cut out of the profits over the Montreal deal. Nevertheless, I had to keep my mouth shut or end up at the bottom of the Detroit River.

You could say that was a forty-four ton diversion. But was it worth the cost? Fifty-six tons made it safely…forty-four tons didn't, so my profit margin dropped immensely, as did Rolf's and the Mob's. Rolf would receive his profit from the Montreal and New York deals. However, I was left holding the bag.

After the twenty percent commission the Mob would receive from the New York deal—that would leave me with less than eighteen tons of "primo" hashish.

To make up the loss, I decided to use the Lebanese sack hash (pollen) and make it like the Afghans did-using fire and water, knead it until I got the consistency needed, then press it into black Afghani-type hashish. Only I would know the difference.

I would get at least two to five thousand dollars a pound, instead of a thousand or less, depending on the quantity being sold, for the sack hash. It would take quite a bit of hard work and time…even so, it would be well worth it. I could make approximately fifty kilos per day, working twelve hour days for two to four weeks, or until Rolf demanded his money.

I felt bad for Rolf losing all that hash, but what the hell, he was a billionaire. His frustration would overcome him and soon turn into anger, as it had for me, Pete, and the others who had expected all three ships to reach port safely. However, Rolf knew the risks. He was lucky to lose only one ship. He could have lost them all and all the money too. It would knock him for a "loop" when he learned of the unexpected loss.

I learned later that Rolf had paid between three and four dollars per kilo for the Lebanese hash, which meant that he had paid less than half-million dollars for the one-hundred ton load. If all three ships had made it into New York Harbor, he would have made more than one hundred times in profit.

Another thing I learned, months later, is why Rolf had picked me to sell his hashish instead of the people he had used and trusted before. His motive was the fact that one person he had known and trusted since his high school years had ripped him off for millions of dollars and Rolf had him tortured and killed. I couldn't believe, through all the talks we had and wires he sent me, that Rolf had a Mob mentality.

In fact, it was two Gambino soldiers who had whacked his trusted friend, and it was the Gambino family who was unloading and trucking the hash to Detroit, even though it was only one-quarter of the amount sent.

Pete and his crew were to make sure that nobody fucked with me. He, Rolf, and I would therefore make money selling the hash and we would get the cash safely to Rolf, even though Rolf would not make the money he had expected; nor would Pete or I.

However, it was Rolf's fault for sending, as the Captain had stated, rusty, old ships that had problems from the time they left Amsterdam. The engine problem should have never happened. Rolf had enough money to purchase either newer or larger ships or, at the very least, replace the engine that caused the problem from the beginning. The Captains knew it and the crewmembers knew it. Evidently, everyone had known except Rolf. Or maybe he just didn't care. One ship getting through the net put out by the Coast Guard would have made him approximately thirty-million, for a half-million dollar scam.

However, to me, thirty million seemed like a hefty sum of money. To the Mob, that was parking meter money, but they weren't happy about the situation at all.

I believe Rolf knew what the outcome would be when the ships and weather didn't perform as they had in previous years. Therefore, I was sure that Rolf knew there was a chance to lose not just one, but all three ships. This was the chance you took in this business.

One question I was certain he would ask himself is why had the Coast Guard picked that particular ship to stop and search? Did one of the ex-crewmembers "rat" him out or was it just luck on the part of the Coast Guard? One thing was for certain: Rolf had no one to blame but himself for the problems that had arisen.

Even so, the ships that carried the contraband safely into port would return to Amsterdam with the money made from selling that same contraband throughout all of Canada and the USA. The Mob would make sure he would receive it. All five NY families had soldiers in all of Europe, including in Amsterdam, and a few soldiers from the Gambino and Bonanno families would travel with the captains on those same ships to make sure that Rolf received his money, minus, of course, the forty million or more that would have been made from the loss of the forty-four ton load.

After payments of large sums of money to the Harbor Master and Customs people, the ship was allowed to be unloaded of the tires. Pete, Sal, Louie, and I watched over Angie Ruggerio and his dockworkers who were doing the unloading, then loading the pallets. Each contained four large tires with wheels that concealed the hashish inside them.

Corallo stayed behind to make sure everything went smoothly, even though Angie was Delecroche's nephew. Delecroche felt disrespect from Corallo, but let it go, not wanting to cause a major rift between the two families. He had left in a huff.

It took over fifteen hours to unload and reload the cargo. Once loaded, the contraband was driven to a warehouse in Queens, which was owned by the Teamsters but run by the Gambino crime Family.

A large number of pallets containing the tires were unloaded and the tires were then disassembled. A total of 4.4 tons of excellent hashish was weighed. This sufficed for the two crime families. Each trailer carried four-hundred and forty pallets, each pallet of four tires contained one-hundred pounds of hashish—twenty-five pounds in each tire.

Before the rest of the load was driven to a Teamster-owned warehouse in Detroit, a few of the workers cut the white linen sacks from the hash to see what they had. The kilo bricks of Lebanese hash were stacked in layers by color, which seemed to be every color of a rainbow. The building reeked of the pungent smell of quality hashish. Seeing that brought back great memories for me of the time I had spent in Afghanistan.

Corallo didn't like the fact that the linen sacks were considered as part of the weight, and couldn't be sold by themselves, so I asked for the sacks that they were going to throw away, which I would have used to make shirts or pants. However, I was completely ignored.

Corallo was frustrated and angry that the 4.4 tons, without the sacks, came to approximately 4.3 tons. I then suggested that they sell the hash with the sacks, as I had to, or lose money.

The hash (or pollen) is placed into linen sacks, weighed, and then pressed in a hydraulic press to make the hash approximately an inch thick, about 14 inches long, in an oval shape, then tied at one end and stamped with each farmers name on the sacks. This is the way the Lebanese pressed their hash for export.

Afghani hash was made differently; pressed by hand or hydraulically in a rectangular metal die after the pollen was placed into a pan of boiling water, dumped onto a plastic sheet, then kneaded by hands and feet. This process went on until the hash was a dark brown all the way through, or black on the outside and green on the inside. It was weighed, usually in kilos, and then pressed. Others made the hash in round patties, about a 1/2" to 1" thick and pressed these by hand, to be either sold to tourists or the Afghans themselves.

Usually, when the Afghans used a hydraulic press, the hash was sold to tourists to be placed in false bottoms of suitcases for smuggling out of the country.

This was the difference in the making of Lebanese and Afghani hashish.

6 CHAPTER

Heading for Detroit

Rolf had purchased ninety percent of the previous year's Lebanese hash crop, which was more than five-hundred tons. The other ten percent had gone to the surrounding Arab countries and its Royal families, Kings, top politicians, and the average Sunni and Shiite citizens.

The Arab countries that purchased Lebanese hashish and tons of opium were mostly Middle Eastern, and included Syria, Egypt, Saudi Arabia, Kuwait, Qatar, Jordan, and other Sunni and Shiite nations of lower means. Part of the Muslim culture is the smoking of superb hashish and eating of opium, usually with their tea.

The Kings and Saudi Royal Families also give the women in their Harems hash, opium, and many other narcotic-type drugs, including uppers and downers. Anything to keep their women happy, which also includes the finest jewelry, diamonds, gold, and other precious and semi-precious stones.

The Royal Family loves beautiful, blond-haired women; ninety-nine percent were foreigners from America, Europe and countries such as Thailand. These women were enticed by the easy money and high life styles that kept these Royal Families happy sexually. The happier they kept these rich oil barons, the more jewelry, gold, diamonds, necklaces and bracelets worth millions of dollars were given to them.

The Royal Families usually made agreements with the women in their harems from advertisements in newspapers and other media outlets (such as websites) or they would buy them in countries like Thailand, India and other third-world countries.

The Golden-Goddesses were the most sought after. Some harems contained fifty or more beautiful women, with healthy, rich severance pay for the women who had grown too old. These women usually returned home multi-millionaires—but enough of harems and Royal history.

Let's get back to the twenty-two ton load.

As the hashish lay stacked on tables, I couldn't wait to get my hands on it. I wanted to tear a kilo in half to really see, smell and feel it, then put a few tads in my hash pipe and smoke it.

As the soldiers of the Gambino and Lucchese families unloaded the pallets, I noticed a few had red "X's" on top of the wrapped plastic covering the tires. I wondered what the "X's" meant. That is, I wondered until the hashish was taken out of the tires. The X-marked hashish was pure black; at least on the outside and seemed to be made similar to the Afghani method. The Mob didn't seem to know this.

A few of the Mafia soldiers placed twenty pallets onto a scale that were used to weigh the trailers before and after they were loaded, and placed the hashish onto them, sacks included, until each pallet had five foot stacks of hashish covering the whole pallet. Amazingly, the total weight of the hashish, minus the weight of the twenty pallets, came up a few kilos shy of the 4.4 tons or twenty percent of the twenty-two tons.

To make sure there were twenty-two tons, the Mafia soldiers used a Hi-Lo and weighed six pallets of Hi-Lo tires, then multiplied the number of each pallet and came up with the tonnage.

After using a wheel and tire changer to get the hashish out of the tires, the Lucchese and Gambino families would use the same machine to put the tires back onto the wheels and then sell them to add to their profits.

The Zerilli family of Detroit would do the same and I promised to give them my tires after they helped me remove the hash to load onto rented panel trucks to distribute to my connections.

Now that the 4.4 tons of hashish had been unloaded, Pete was anxious, as was I, to get the rest of the load of contraband to Detroit so we could start selling it. Unlike the Gambino Family, the Zerilli Family had no qualms about selling illegal drugs, whether it was heroin, cocaine, hashish, or stolen prescription narcotic drugs of every type, including upper and downers: Anything to make a buck.

Nine hours after delivering the hashish to the warehouse in Queens, NY, Corallo told Pete, "I believe I found the people that tried to kill you and your soldiers."

"Yeah, and who may that be?"

"It was Castellano and one of his crew, led by a man named Roy DeMayo. Evidently, Castellano was angry that he had been kept out of the deal and may have been the person who notified the Coast Guard about the ships."

Pete replied, "If your information is true, Don Corallo, I will, I swear, get my revenge and don't give a flying fuck if Castellano is an underboss of the Gambino Family or not."

Corallo nodded.

Pete then yelled to the truck drivers, "All right, let's get this hash to Detroit."

The tractor-trailers drove out of the Queens Warehouse and finally made it to the Teamster's warehouse just outside of Detroit fourteen hours later.

That's when I learned that my Uncle's favor would cost me another twenty percent of the remaining load. To say the least, I was very upset. I could do nothing though, but allow him to take his share of the shipment.

After Pete and his Mob received his twenty percent, I would be left with 13.2 tons. So, my cut, after selling Rolf's half, would be 6.6 tons, instead of the fifty tons I was to get originally, with Rolf getting the same amount.

I had really screwed this deal up when I had asked the Mob for their help. The three Mob Families, Gambino, Lucchese and Zerilli, made forty percent combined, while Rolf and I made thirty percent each. I was completely taken by surprise over this unforeseen action.

However, Rolf would make eighty-percent on the thirty-three tons that reached the Port of Montreal, after the Bonanno and other two families made their twenty percent.

I was left out of that deal. Make no mistake about it though, I would make plenty of money from the tonnage I had to sell. If all went well, that was.

I was even more upset when Pete allowed me only two weeks to get the hash out of the warehouse to my safe-houses, even though Pete would transport the load of hash to the designated area. I decided upon using his rig. This meant that I had to work fast and pay Pete and his thugs to get the hash out of the tires before I could transport it to my friend's farmhouse in Northern Michigan, called "Sun Farms." I had to weigh it and transport one hundred pound loads or more in each rented panel truck.

I had the "Brotherhood" in California ready to purchase one or two tons, depending on the price, and I would be responsible for the transportation from Michigan to California. They wanted to buy it for two hundred dollars per pound; I wanted five hundred.

Once I had distributed the rest to my other friends and connections, I would take a half ton of hash to my place and turn the Lebanese into Affy. That would take at least two weeks or even longer. However, I would sell that hash after selling the Lebanese, and that would be clear profit for me; at the very least two-thousand dollars per pound. I was hoping to clear at least one or more million from that deal.

We had a hell of a lot of work to do, unloading the pallets of tires from the trailers, so we began the work immediately. After only a few hard hours of work, we picked different spaces inside the building and we lay down on pallets of grain sacks; anything that would give us as much comfort as possible. There were clean beds for the truckers to use while waiting for their cargo to be loaded onto their trucks, but those were off limits to us. We all made do, though.

After all this work, I had to do some morphine. I went into one of the bathroom stalls and took out my "fix kit." No one was in the bathroom, so I quickly took out my spoon, placed two half-grain tablets into it, added a little bit of hot tap water and, within ten seconds, the morphine dissolved. Placing a little ball of cotton into the spoon, I then sucked the drug into my syringe. I went into a stall, wrapped my belt around my right arm and shoved the needle into my main vein. I pulled the syringe until blood flowed into it, unloosened the belt and shot the morphine into my body. Instantaneously, I got the rush I craved. I sat down on the toilet seat for a few minutes until the rush subsided. It felt heavenly, like I was in "Never, Never Land." I quickly cleaned my works and spoon and then went to my bed of grain and fell asleep.

Soon, we heard the roar of diesel engines. The trucks left the warehouse within an hour, most heading north; some going all the way to the far parts of Alaska. Thank God these trucks had nothing to do with our loads.

A few hours later, our trucks were ready for the ride to Detroit. After the three families took their forty percent, that left me with 13.2 tons to sell. Minus Rolf's share, I was left with 6.6 tons.

As we said our "Goodbyes" to the Goombas, Pete, Sal, Louie, and I got into Pete's Caddy (with me driving of course).

"Follow those 'Big Rigs'," Pete ordered, "And be prepared for anything." As the three tractor-trailers left the warehouse, Pete reminded his soldiers, "Be ready for any action that might come our way; you never know when a firefight might ensue."

They quickly pulled their weapons from under their suit coats, just in case we were shot at and the trucks hijacked. For the next hour, we were at the height of our senses, looking all around for any and all vehicles that looked suspicious.

To say the least, I was very nervous. I had gone through a near death experience earlier and didn't want it to happen again. Luckily for us, nothing out of the ordinary happened.

The farther we drove the calmer I became; taking a valium had a lot to do with that.

Within a short time, we were in Pennsylvania, on the toll roads and every time we had to pay the toll, Pete bitched and bitched and bitched and usually had Sal drop the money into the toll machine.

During the ride to Detroit, Pete opened up and began telling me of the Mob's business, especially the drug business. He began telling me about the connections they had made throughout the world and how they transported the narcotics from Thailand, Turkey, and also Columbia, via Brazil.

I was mostly interested in the methods they used to smuggle liquid morphine base into one of three countries, to be turned into pure 99.9% heroin to sell on the streets of America. The methods used were quite ingenious. They bought the opium from the Turkish Military, and then the Mob took the truckloads of opium to their chemists to change it into morphine base. This was more hassle than buying pure heroin made by Burmese chemists (Burma is now named Myanmar), which was then smuggled into Thailand to sell to the buyers.

Three of the five NY Families were involved in these transactions as was the Detroit Mafia. They had certain soldiers from each family send six month old diesel Mercedes equipped with fifty gallon fuel tanks via cargo container ships to their particular destinations. In Turkey, the opium was turned into liquid morphine, poured into the cars' gas tanks, along with a gallon or so of pure alcohol. By modifying the fuel injection system with a hidden fuel line, which returned the morphine to the gas tank, the diesel engine then ran on the alcohol.

Usually these cars were towed or driven less than a mile to the docks, then loaded into a special container on a cargo ship, which set sail for the NY docks. Once the cars passed customs, they were taken to a large warehouse to have the gas tanks removed. Mob chemists then changed fifty gallons of liquid morphine into approximately six kilos of pure white 99% heroin.

The Thai operation went much faster because the opium did not have to be converted into morphine and then to heroin. That one step in the process saved weeks in the operation. The smuggled heroin was mixed with alcohol, again placed into the Mercedes gas tanks, and using the special fitting fuel adapter to the fuel injection system, the heroin would return to the fuel tank while the engine drove on the alcohol. The cars were loaded into cargo containers, which were then loaded onto ships that were bound for the NY docks, where the Mob had complete control.

Once the cargo containers were Ok'd by customs, they were loaded onto forty-foot tractor-trailers to be taken to a special warehouse to claim the product. The cars were unloaded, the gas tanks removed, and then the chemists took control of the product.

Evaporating the alcohol from the cars sent from Thailand was much easier and faster, and left nearly 47 to 50 kilos of pure white 99% heroin per car to be distributed around the country. The Mob used at least thirty cars every month loaded with this contraband, which added up to approximately 1600 kilos of 99% heroin. Adding the cars used from the Turkish operation and that put the approximate total weight of heroin at more than 1800 kilos of pure heroin. This still didn't include the heroin that was sent through Columbian connections. Adding the tons of cocaine that were bought from the cartels, Pete and his Mob alone were selling quite a few tons of powders, which meant "mucho dinero."

As we left the warehouse, I asked Pete why he sent used cars back to America instead of new cars. His answer was that "new cars had to be checked, taxed, and fees were added. Cars that were at least six months old were considered an old car and not taxed or fined." I thought to myself; *that made sense*. And using their US, Thai, and Turkish customs connections meant no risk of jail or execution.

Before the big drug epidemic, many of the soldiers returning from Vietnam were addicted to 100% heroin made by the Chinese Military chemists and given to the North Vietnamese military to be used strictly for the purpose of addicting our troops. Three of the five Mafia families saw a chance to get in on the action by using a few four-star Generals and CIA operatives as mules because they owed thousands of dollars in gambling debts. These mules transported two to three kilos of pure heroin from Vietnam every month to the good old US of A until their debts were paid, which amounted to approximately sixty kilos.

However, the Mob wanted more and this meant that they had to change their smuggling methods. They moved on to different heroin producing countries, such as the Golden Triangle.

That's where the Mob came up with the idea of using cars to smuggle heroin. They wanted to continue to smuggle heroin from Vietnam, but unfortunately a black drug dealer from Harlem beat them to the punch. He was their biggest competitor and used American military aircraft to smuggle in tons of 100% heroin bought from the Chinese and Vietnamese cartels run by their military hierarchy.

During this time, the streets of New York and elsewhere were flooded with pure heroin called "Blue Magic." The stuff was so good that the average citizen began experimenting with the drug, not with the needle, but by snorting it up their noses. As pure as it was, within a few days of use, they became addicted. This made the five Mafia families angry because the cost of heroin dropped sharply, which meant that the Mob was losing millions of dollars due to this unfortunate circumstance.

Therefore, the Mob put a hit out on the black dealer. However, the war was winding down and the big time dealer from Harlem had lost his Vietnam connections. Before the Mob could whack him, the FEDS and DEA got to him first and he was given a life sentence. Nevertheless, the damage had been done.

First time users who were sold pure heroin were now addicted to the drug, which the mob was glad to supply. Now, instead of buying pure heroin, the Mob added other chemicals to the drug, which made the user buy more and more of the product. This caused a crime wave across the country, just from the addicts trying to get the money to sustain their habits.

The Government saw the addiction rate to heroin explode, so they had the states open up Methadone clinics. This got the addicts off the needle, but now they were addicted to Methadone. Many states used liquid Methadone so that the addicts could slowly decrease their dose until they were drug free.

By this time, cocaine was the rage. The Mafia had connections with the Columbian cartels to buy as much cocaine as needed. In the beginning, they used the same method as they had to smuggle heroin—the used Mercedes. However, they couldn't smuggle enough of the drug to satisfy the growing American market. Therefore, they came up with another means of smuggling that worked not only for cocaine but also for excellent pot.

The three Mafia families that were in the business of selling addicting powders invested millions of dollars to buy used American Military aircraft; mainly cargo planes. Once modified to their specifications, these planes could fly from Pennsylvania to the jungles of Columbia.

THE AGE OF AQUARIUS II

While the mechanics modified the aircraft, the Mob began hiring ex-military pilots who had flown the same type of aircraft during the Vietnam War. Carrying a full load of contraband from Columbia to America, the pilots could earn more money than if they had flown fifty tours in Vietnam. In fact, the Mob hired more pilots than they had aircraft, just to be on the safe side.

Once the project started, tons of pot and cocaine were coming in regularly; approximately five loads a day. This went on for quite a few years, until one of the planes crashed within a few miles of the runway and burned. The pilot lived to tell his tales, and he did, to the FEDS, to keep his ass out of prison.

This situation caused the Mob to change their landing zones, both in Columbia and America.

The loads continued, but their methods of smuggling the drugs changed. Instead of five loads per day, it went to three, two, and then one. When the American Military and Coast Guard became involved in operations to stop the drug smuggling, this put a kink in the Mobs' ways.

The Mob, however, always seemed to be one step ahead of the FEDS. Nothing was going to stop their smuggling and hijacking.

The Sicilian Mafia had been smuggling and hijacking in Sicily for hundreds of years. Now they had a much larger country in which to continue their way of life.

When the American Military became involved in the "Drug War," the Mob returned to their old ways of smuggling cocaine from Columbia and heroin from the same countries they had used before, using their main connections. They decided to forgo smuggling pot from Columbia because the profit margin was too little for the risk involved.

Consequently, for a time, pot was nearly impossible to buy. That was, until I mentioned that they should grow it themselves, in their soldiers' basements. Pete liked the idea and passed it on to Giacalone, who was given the "go ahead" from the Don.

I provided the seeds and showed them how to grow it and they took it from there. To this day, many people call me "Johnny Appleseed," and I take pride in that name. Now half the American population is growing pot; either for their own use or to sell, while many states are allowing pot for medical purposes. All because of what I started. And soon, with so many people out of work, the states are likely to legalize it; that is if Congress passes the Commerce Act to enact the legalization of growing and selling the stuff.

I'm sure the politicians will act upon this soon because the country needs money. Every state is bankrupt and 70 million citizens smoke it. This would put America back in the black. Not only is pot non-addictive, it also relieves the pain caused by many diseases. Besides, if it wasn't a useful plant, God wouldn't have created it.

#

Finally, after twelve long hours, we made it to the warehouse in Detroit. It was a long ride, but Pete kept us awake with his tales of the history of the Mafia and how it was just a business. He explained it as if the Mob was doing the citizens of the world a favor by giving them what the US Government wouldn't; like during the prohibition days. The Government banned liquor, so the Mob stepped in and sold it to the people who wanted it.

We decided to sleep at the warehouse that night so we could get a fresh start the next day to unload the tractor-trailers and get the hash out of the tires.

7

CHAPTER

Unloading the contraband

After a good night's sleep and a decent breakfast, we were ready for a few days of hard work. Once the warehouse workers showed up, Pete instructed them to unload the three trailers full of tires, take them to the tire changing machine, as we had done in New York City, and remove the hashish.

"Aren't you worried about these guys ratting us out?" I asked Pete.

"Nah," he answered. "They're paid too well to do something that dumb. Not to worry."

The workers were affiliated with the Mob, so this wasn't anything unusual and Pete had use of the warehouse for seven days. After that, we had to get out and leave no evidence behind. Within those seven days, we had to unload the tires, get the contraband out, put the tires back onto the rims, and load the hash into one trailer and the tires onto the other. To do this, meant that we would have to work continuously until the job was finished. If we couldn't eat or sleep for those seven days, so be it. Those were Pete's orders and you didn't disobey them, or bad things would happen to you.

We awoke at 6 a.m.; the workers arrived ten minutes later. After Pete gave the orders, everyone went to work, even Pete.

Once the rear doors of the trucks were opened, four Hi-Los and their drivers were anxious to begin removing the pallets; there were two Hi-Los per trailer and the pallets were then placed near each side of the machine that removed the tires from the rims.

Four workers did that job in four-hour shifts. One person removed the tire by placing a special tapered 14 inch piece of hardened steel between the rim and the tire. Then, as the man stepped on a hydraulic jack, the hardened steel pressed down and circled the tire, pushing the edge of the tire over the rim, freeing the tire from the rim. The same would be done to the other side of the tire. It took two people to do that job.

Once the tire was removed from the machine, the worker then reached into it and removed ten to fifteen sacks of hash, depending on the weight of each sack.

One man would then place the tire back over the rim, and this process was reversed to replace the tire back onto the rim. Two men then took the tire off the machine and placed it onto a pallet. The hash was weighed, recorded into an accounting book and then placed into 4ft. x 4ft. x 4ft. cardboard boxes, each of which weighed approximately one hundred pounds when full. This was then put onto a Hi-Lo and stacked onto a tractor-trailer.

This process continued for nearly three days and filled more than thirteen tons, or 26,400 pounds, of some of the sweetest hashish in the world that I was about to have the privilege to sell since my Afghani days.

Of course, Pete took his twenty percent, which netted him 4.4 tons; the same as the two Mafia families were given. He was ecstatic over the amount he was given for what little work he had done and he allowed me to sell his share.

Man, it gave me goose bumps just looking at the different colors of the hash (or as the Afghani's called it:

powder.) There were at least a dozen different colors, from white to black, and all shades in between.

We also had many more pallets with the red "X" on them that contained the black, primo hashish than the New York boys had gotten.

Pete allowed me to keep all the hash from the pallets marked with the "X." This would sell as Afghani hashish and make two to three times as much as the Lebanese.

One fifth of the warehouse was full of hundreds of tires and rims. Hundreds of boxes of hash were then loaded into the three tractor-trailers and driven to "Sun Farms" for safekeeping.

Only four people, myself included, unloaded and stacked the boxes into my friend's (Greg) three-story barn. That job took us nearly twelve hours and our net at the end totaled more than twenty-six-thousand pounds in twelve foot high stacks.

The "X" I had placed on two sides of twenty boxes indicated that they contained the Affy-type hashish. The others contained different shades of red, green, brown and white.

A quarter of Greg's barn was filled with my hash. He also owned the farm and wanted to throw a large party to celebrate this unique occasion, but I refused. I did not want to bring attention to my score until most of it was sold.

To sooth his feelings, I allowed him to pick out one box of his choosing for risking his life and farm. Wouldn't you know it; he picked out a box that had the "X" on it. I agreed, even though I wanted that hash for myself.

As quickly as I nodded my head, he brought down a box and opened it. The room filled with a sensual aroma: A pungent, sweet smell.

He tore away the sack, a one inch thick by a 14" oval, then broke the slab in half onto a clean newspaper, where little tads of hash spilled onto it. Like magic, he had a small hash pipe in his hand and a lighter. He began picking up the hash that fell onto the newspaper, grabbed a few small chunks, then placed them into his pipe and lit God's given high.

As Greg began coughing and spitting up from the pungent and strong smoke, he just lay back on the straw on the floor of his barn and passed the pipe to me. I too took a strong toke on the pipe and did exactly as Greg had. I could have sworn this hash was from Afghanistan, but I knew it wasn't. It was Lebanese hash, but had the high of Afghani.

All we needed was that one toke. Finally, after nearly ten minutes, we picked ourselves up from the floor and, in unison, said, "Fuck, that is some good shit!"

We both laughed. Grabbing the two slabs of hash from the newspaper, we went into his house and started making plans to get rid of the goods: fast and at a good price.

It took us another two hours before we returned to the barn and opened up a few other boxes without the "X" on them. We couldn't believe our eyes. The first box opened had three different shades of green: light, medium and dark. Each had the same potent smell and weighed approximately the same as the black hash.

Greg and I were full of happiness. Had I been a reindeer, my nose would have lit up red like Rudolf's.

We opened a few other boxes with different shades of different colors. One had different shades of red: light, medium and dark; the same with the brown and the white. I had only seen a few different colors in Afghanistan: Mostly green "powder" or a dark brown. Very rarely would I see white "powder."

Since I had stopped sending hashish from Afghanistan, it was hard to find. Now we had more than we knew what to do with.

After discussing the situation for another hour, while smoking the black hash, we wrote down names and phone numbers of people we would be distributing it to and we came up with a price. If the buyer were to buy a ton or more, I would sell it for five hundred dollars per pound, including the sack.

THE AGE OF AQUARIUS II

Less than that, the prices would go up, depending on the potency and color. White hash was very rare to find. I had sent some to America from Afghanistan on special occasions, like Christmas and Easter, to which opium was added.

Once we had made a list of business associates to contact, we returned to the barn, grabbed about thirty pounds of every color of hash and brought it into the house. Then we began making phone calls.

The first call was made to Greg's partner, Jeremy, the head honcho and bigwig in this business. Jeremy was a true business man. He sold hash and his Columbian pot for one purpose: to make money.

The reason I sent hash from Afghanistan was so my friends could smoke the best hash in the world. The money I made I gave away to the poor Afghan kids who couldn't afford shoes or coats in the wintertime. That's the main reason why I returned to America broke.

At the time of the telephone call, Jeremy was in California making new connections to sell his pot. When he heard about this score, he flew home as fast as he could. Within six hours, he had returned from California.

We picked him up at the airport, and began driving to "Sun Farms." Greg had a few grams of different colors of hash to show his partner. Once Jeremy saw and smoked some, he was ecstatic.

A few hours later, we had arrived at the farm. Jeremy was in a hurry to see the tons of hash. He was as giddy as a little school kid.

He wanted to sell as much as I would allow, so we agreed on a price of four-hundred dollars per pound; a hundred dollars cheaper than I had wanted to sell it.

He mentioned that his connections would be interested in a ton or more; about the same as my connections. However, that meant we still had more than ten or eleven tons left to sell.

I figured I could sell four or five hundred pounds to each of the four cities to which I had distributed in my younger years and much more to my connections in California.

After talking business for the next few hours and deciding on what we were going to do, we each began calling our connections.

I first called the "Brotherhood of Eternal Love," who did their business mainly in California. They couldn't wait to get here and promised to buy one or more tons, depending on the quality and price. I told them they wouldn't be disappointed. They decided to catch a plane that very same day and be the first ones in line. Once they purchased the promised amount, they would truck their load themselves, using a rental tractor-trailer.

With that call completed, I dropped another "dime" and called a dealer closer to home to tell him the news.

Greg and Jeremy were also calling their connections to their dealers.

The first of their dealers came over within an hour, from Ann Arbor. When they saw thirty pounds of primo hash and the rainbow of colors, they couldn't buy it fast enough. They decided on a box of red and a box of green hash, which weighed a little over two hundred pounds.

The price negotiated was seven hundred dollars per pound. That meant I would receive four hundred dollars for each pound sold, which would earn Rolf and myself our first $80,000: $40,000 for each of us.

The process was completed within less than an hour and Greg's dealers were on their way to their abode, stating that "they would return within a day or two."

I wasn't too happy with the transaction. I only made $80,000 dollars on the deal. Greg and Jeremy were ecstatic. They made $60,000 on the deal. Not too bad for an hour's work. However, if I continued to keep the stash at their farm, I wouldn't make the kind of money needed to give Rolf his due.

THE AGE OF AQUARIUS II

I knew then that I had to move the hash to another setting or Rolf would make a pittance of what we had decided upon. However, there were over 243 boxes to move and that would take some time. I had to figure a way to move the one-hundred-pound boxes to another stash house or to make another deal with Greg and Jeremy: Something to the effect of offering them a total of one-thousand pounds to sell at $400 dollars per pound, not including the black hash.

Jeremy was very headstrong and would be the person who would give me the most trouble. Greg I could deal without a problem; we had gone to school together and at one time hung around. That is, until he hooked up with Jeremy, who, in my eyes, was just a young smart ass kid who came from a rich family and had the money to help Greg build a small business into a much larger one, faster than expected.

I thought about having Pete whack the two guys and then I would have the farm to myself and my problems would end, but that idea didn't sit too well with me. I knew Pete and his crew would have no problem whacking them, but what would it cost me? And if that did go down, Pete would own me for life. He already had his nails stuck into me. I didn't want to take the chance of making my "bones" for him and being indebted to him for life. And that is what would happen if it were to go that far.

I was in a "Catch 22." Instead of thinking about it, I decided to party with Greg, Jeremy, and his friends who had bought the hash. That took my mind off my problem —and it worked. That is, until the following morning—then the problem was still with me.

Greg and Jeremy were continuously on the phone, calling their top drug distributors, trying to sell my hash as quickly as possible. However, the more they sold at the price I gave them for stashing my hash at their farm, the more both Rolf and I were losing, and losing big money.

Three hundred pounds wasn't a big factor out of 26,100 pounds, which was what I had left to sell after giving

Greg one hundred pounds for stashing the product at his farm and taking into account the two hundred pounds they had just sold.

Jeremy was now talking with a connection in California for nearly a ton of my hash. He wanted an even cheaper price for selling that amount, but I refused, telling him four hundred was the lowest I could go. Then, out of the blue he became the "bastard" I always knew he was and began threatening me to either sell the hash to him at his price or I could take my "shit" and get it off his farm within the next two days. He went on to say that my hash was going to "ruin his pot business."

I couldn't believe my ears. He was making good money from selling my hash and **it** was "ruining his pot business."

Even Greg was dumbfounded. He was more than satisfied with the deal I had given them and didn't understand Jeremy's reasoning. "Jeremy, you're talking out your ass," he said.

Jeremy continued to rant and rave, saying, "I don't mean to be such a prick or hard ass, but Greg was an idiot to allow you to stash that much hash on our farm. If we get caught, not only will all of us go to the slammer for the rest of our lives, but we'll lose the farm, our connections, and everything we own."

Greg spoke up, saying, "I told Robert that he could keep the hash here for at least a week. In fact, he has the Brotherhood of Eternal Love coming in from California promising to buy at least two tons if not more. Hell, the shit has only been here for two days and, by tomorrow, his buyers will be here with cash. They promised Willingham that if the hash was as good as he promised, they would buy possibly three tons and return for more."

Greg's argument was reasonable, but wasn't expected.

I thought Greg was the boss of this outfit, but after listening to Jeremy's diatribe, I knew then that Jeremy controlled the business, even though Greg was a year older and had brought Jeremy into the business.

I thought Jeremy would be pleased. Unfortunately that wasn't the case. It was all right to have three tons of Columbian pot on Greg's farm, but because I was now invading Jeremy's privacy, he didn't like it.

You could say I was a little "pissed off" listening to a "greedy" Jeremy. However, I still had one trick up my sleeve that Jeremy wasn't aware of: My Uncle Pete and his soldiers. All I had to do was make one phone call to Pete and my problems would go away.

I then decided my only way out of this trouble was to call him and have the boxes picked up, using four of his soldiers and his tractor-trailer. But where would I take this huge amount of hash? I really had no place to put it, other than at the farm, and if I did that, I would have to tell Greg and Jeremy that I would have to sell it to them at a much higher price. That way, Rolf would get the money he deserved from what was left of the twenty-two ton load. Then I thought about the hundred ton load. Where in the hell would I have put it if I had no help from anyone?

The Mob had already taken forty percent of the twenty-two ton cargo.

Greg and Jeremy thought they could sell as much as they wanted and throw a "bone" my way. That wasn't going to work; not in my book, anyway.

I again thought about Pete and his crew whacking them and then I would have the farm to myself. Two hundred pounds wasn't a big factor. However, if they began selling tons, then it would be a big factor. I wasn't about to let that happen; so I decided to make a special call to my Uncle Pete to ask him to have a sit-down with my two competitors and straighten them out and read them the riot act. Pete saw no problem with that; in fact, he rather liked the idea of me needing his help and another favor. So he and three of his "Goombas" arrived at the farm early the following morning.

CHAPTER 8

Close Calls; Hashish sold; Millions made

Pete, Sal, Louie and a guy I didn't know, who went by the name of "Killer," arrived at the farm around 7 a.m. in Pete's Caddy. That told me the hashish wasn't going anywhere unless I wanted it to.

Jeremy and Greg were sleeping, knocked out by the quantity of liquor, hash, and other drugs, namely cocaine and valium.

They were quite surprised when two very large soldiers of Pete's crew kicked in their bedroom doors and smacked their faces until they were aware of what was happening. To say the least, they had no idea what these large fellows wanted.

I could hear Jeremy whining. He told Sal and Louie, "Take whatever you want, but just leave us alive to live another day."

Both Sal and Louie laughed at that one.

Jeremy was so overwhelmed by the 'Goombas' behavior that he actually pissed his underwear. Urine flowed onto the sixteenth-century handmade mattress of his French Canopy bed.

THE AGE OF AQUARIUS II

Jeremy tried to pull his nine-millimeter pistol from underneath his pillow. However, before he could fire it, Sal came up from behind and cold-cocked him on the back of his head. That opened up about a three-inch gash on the right side of his head. Once he came to, Jeremy was begging for his life and offering them pretty much everything he had in his home, except for the hidden money in off-shore accounts in the Cayman Islands.

After a few hours of threats and torture, he gave up the accounting books without another problem, which had approximately fifty-four million in just that one account. Within a few more hours, he gave up every hidden off shore bank account, worth nearly three-quarters of a billion dollars. He also gave up his contacts throughout the world, including his cocaine and pot connections, which included a powerful politician named Pablo Escobar from the city of Medellin, Columbia and many powerful military officials who were paid by the Mexican Government to stop the flow of illegal narcotics, but instead were in bed with the Cartels, whose families went back hundreds of years.

When I heard this, it actually made me sick, because I had allowed him to take over the four cities that I once controlled, which helped him become a billionaire.

For a kid of twenty-four years old, he had some pretty powerful connections in the drug industry and was still alive. How he did it I don't know. I do know, however, that he was playing with fire. It was just a matter of time before he succumbed to the scourge of these powerful drug lords.

Jeremy was ordered by Pete to introduce these powerful drug connections to him and the New York commission. In return, Jeremy and Greg were allowed to live.

I never knew that Jeremy and Greg had such powerful drug connections or how they came about getting them. I did it in Afghanistan, but the hierarchy of the Afghan Government was a small circle of corrupt relatives and very close friends, including one of the King's Uncles, who allowed the flow of opium to be delivered by the truckload from the Badakhsan and Helmand provinces, while the hashish was grown in the Balkh province and allowed to flow into the city of Kabul and other nearby cities. The police and military taxed these truckloads of contraband, and that money was then divided up between their top officers and Generals.

It seemed nearly all the countries, including America, worked the same way.

Since Pete had straightened out my problem, Jeremy, Greg and I had come to an understanding and were again friends. Not close friends, but "friends." I allowed them to sell as much of my hash as they could, at four-hundred dollars per pound.

Pete, however, told them in the strictest of terms that if there were any more hassles between us, the Sun Farm's twosome would be buried on their farm and before their deaths, they would sign over the deed to the property to him. I knew Pete was very serious. Killing was just a business to him and his thugs.

Guns were a non-entity to us. We were peaceniks, not killers. Even though I had dealt with the Mob during this score and had met some scary killers, whom you might call psychopaths and who had killed twenty to thirty people, Pete's "Goombas" were no different.

I saw it up close during the fiasco in Cleveland over the try at Bobby Green. These types of guys weren't playing with a full deck.

Greg and Jeremy evidently got the message and took Pete's threat seriously because there weren't any problems after that. I could tell, however, that they didn't want me around anymore and didn't speak with me much after Pete and his soldiers did their thing. However, now they had no choice. I was calling the "shots."

Sometime that afternoon, my two friends from the "Brotherhood of Love," John the Samoan and Tim Stoneman

THE AGE OF AQUARIUS II

(I never knew Stoneman's first name in Kabul or the Samoan's last name), came to the farm with three suitcases full of cash.

They quickly picked out their boxes of hash, which equaled not two but three tons, including two boxes marked "X." They rented a tractor-trailer and drove the load to Marine County themselves.

I sold the hash to them for five-hundred per pound and gave them one box marked "X" for free. They gave me a total of three million dollars, all in fifties and one-hundred-dollar bills. That left me with less than twenty thousand pounds to sell and a heavy load of cash. However, Pete took most of the money an hour after it was delivered.

Pete had a number of his soldiers stay at the farm until the last remnants of the hash was sold. During their stay, I transported what was left of the boxes marked "X" to my basement and a number of other boxes, which I stashed until I could make them into an Afghani reproduction.

I had more than one ton of different varieties transferred by truck to my basement and another ton split equally between two other close friends. I wanted to wait until there was a lull in the hash business and then bring out the so-called Affy, to be sold at two-thousand per pound.

Jeremy and Greg, even though they felt raped after being threatened by my Uncle and his thugs, continued to sell a number of tons of hash at the four-hundred dollars per pound price.

And my friends from California returned to Michigan for another three tons. Hash was supposedly hard to come by and their distributors wanted as much as they could get. Most of it they made into hash oil and the rest was sold as is for nearly two-thousand dollars per pound.

Pot was very cheap and plentiful in certain parts of California, but hashish was nearly a non-entity and was bought up as soon as it was put on market. Soon after, pot was hard to get, with cocaine being the drug of choice. The "Heads," though, still wanted that heavy hash buzz.

The disco scene was big in Southern California, and with that came cocaine at $100.00 per gram, which was cut so badly that the people who purchased it were only getting maybe 10% coke and the rest was cut. Nevertheless, people still bought it and every so often, a purer variety from Peru would be the rage, which brought prices down and quality up. However, these same coke heads bought hash to bring them down from the coke, so they could sleep and not stay up all night.

It took me nearly a month to sell all 26,400 pounds of hash, minus the 2 tons I took instead of money.

In fact, before leaving the warehouse in Detroit, Pete took me aside and explained that hash wasn't his forte and he had me sell his four tons at two-hundred dollars per pound because he couldn't sell that large a quantity. He was afraid the cops or Feds would search his house for other reasons and find his stash of hash. I agreed with his proposition to be responsible and to keep his cut at the farm, to which he agreed.

Pete was more at ease selling the powders. That was his money maker. Pure heroin at that time was going for 30 to 50 grand a kilo and cocaine was selling at 70 grand per kilo. That is, until the cartels began shipping the shit in cargo containers carrying nearly ten tons at a time, which dropped the price immensely.

Nearly 9 out of 10 young adults were doing coke instead of heroin, because they believed it wasn't addicting and they could snort it instead of injecting it into their veins. The drug world began changing, slowly at first, until there wasn't enough to supply all the users.

Pot had nearly disappeared from radar and coke was the cool thing to use, especially to pick up chicks; they couldn't get enough of the drug, which they used to lose weight and to party at the discos.

While everyone was doing coke, I wasn't. I had seen what it had done to the cocaine addicts of Asia and Europe. Despite that, every one of my friends who were doing the drug said it wasn't addictive, and if it was it was "psychologically addictive," that they could quit any time, without going through withdrawals, as you did after being hooked on heroin.

I knew better. One girl came to mind, and that was Uffy, a girl from France whom I had met in Kabul and used as a whore for my customs contacts. She injected pharmaceutical cocaine made either in Peru or Bolivia; this stuff was one hundred percent pure. Along with injecting the cocaine, she also added a half-grain tablet of pure morphine to mellow out the heavy rush, which she called a "speedball."

In Kabul, I purchased a three gram vial of one-hundred percent Peruvian Coke, which was a golden color, for less than three dollars. Bolivian cocaine was white as snow. This was the first and last time I ever injected the drug. With the Peruvian cocaine, I nearly overdosed on just a match-head; that's how strong the drug was. I promised myself I would never do cocaine again, at least never inject it.

Three days later, Mark left for Pakistan to renew his Afghan visa. I stayed behind; and during this time I met three Italians living together: two guys from Venice named Phillip and Antonio who claimed to be teachers, who had been kicked out of their country for being Revolutionaries, and a beautiful, red-headed American girl from New Jersey who had married Philip.

I noticed one night while visiting my new friends that they were injecting a dark liquid into their syringes. They called it opium and they had bought it in Kandahar. Unfortunately for me, they talked me into injecting the drug into my vein.

After the cocaine debacle, I refused, but after some sweet talking from the beautiful redhead, I relented to her suggestion. She injected the drug into my vein and suddenly a euphoric feeling rushed through my entire body, from my head to my toes. The rush was indescribable.

Afterwards, I wished I had never done the drug because it took complete control of my mind and body; and with the help of my Italian friends, I continued to use it on a daily basis. I couldn't stop myself. The feeling the drug had over me was pure "heaven; an eternal glow that warmed my body through and through. I struggled with my inner feelings not to inject the drug. However, the euphoric rush won over my struggle. From that day forward, I wanted to feel that heavenly feeling daily.

I was a rookie at injecting opium, so I had Antonio move into my room and every cool morning, as soon as I awoke, I had him inject me with the drug until the opium was depleted.

He told me about a drug called "morphine," which I could buy in small bottles from a pharmacy not too far from our hotel. A bottle contained twenty, one-hundred-percent, half-grain tablets per bottle at a cost of three American dollars. He also explained how much more potent the morphine tablets were than the opium. I couldn't refuse his offer and bought a total of ten bottles.

I was very anxious to try this new drug, basically to see if it was as potent and good as Antonio promised. He was true to his word. The half-grain morphine tablets had an even better high than the opium.

Now, I had Antonio inject me with the morphine. I must say, the rush was twice that of the opium, euphorically speaking of course.

I knew this was the drug for me and, after a week, Antonio showed me how to inject the drug myself. That was the drug and habit I returned with, keeping the secret to myself and especially not wanting Pete to know.

Even though Pete was selling heroin, I believed that drug to be the "Devil's drug," one that you couldn't escape from. Pharmaceutical morphine, however, was OK in my mind, because it was made by a pharmaceutical company and one-hundred-percent pure.

9

CHAPTER

The Hash is sold; Rolf gets his money.

My good friend, Al, was the person I had sent five envelopes of hash the first time I visited Kabul and I received all five a week later. When I returned from Afghanistan and went to his house, he gave me half of the hash I had sent.

From that day, I knew he could be trusted and I stashed a thousand pounds in his basement for safekeeping. Fortunately he sold it before the run-in with two motorcycle thugs who kicked in his front door, while another of our friends, John D., was visiting him.

As the thugs tried coming through the door, Al pulled out his .357 and killed them with precise shooting, with the same confidence he had used in the fields of Vietnam.

We were lucky that the cops never searched his house and found the few pounds he had stashed for his personal use.

After speaking with him for nearly an hour, he gave me four hundred thousand dollars: My profit at four hundred per pound.

My other friend, John D., who had the other thousand pounds of hash stashed in his basement, had sold his for more than one thousand per pound in a short period of time; and those who bought it were only too happy to give him their money because there wasn't any "smoke" to be found. I received the same amount of money as I had from Al.

Jeremy and Greg were no longer trusted friends. They had become competitors once again and were making accusations against me for reasons unknown. I surmised that they hadn't approved of my call to my Uncle Pete to help straighten out our differences. It had to be done, or someone might have gotten hurt; and I didn't want it to come to that.

Even so, once John's hash had been sold, that was the last of the 22 ton shipment from Amsterdam, except for the ton I had and I wasn't about to come out with that until people were begging for it.

Everyone was doing powders: cocaine mainly. Snorting the product was the preferred method of ninety-nine percent of the customers. Others were injecting it, but only if it was pure; and pure cocaine was hard to come by and very expensive. Most of the supposed cocaine addicts were actually snorting or shooting methamphetamine, which was easy to tell because it had a gasoline smell and taste to it.

When I told my friends this, they didn't believe me and suggested it was nearly pure cocaine because you only had to snort a small portion of the drug. I knew better, after buying pure pharmaceutical cocaine in Afghanistan. However, I couldn't convince my friends that they were doing **speed**, a drug that ate away your organs from the inside out and would leave large sores all over their bodies with continued use.

Approximately two months after selling the twenty or so tons of hash, the country was completely dry of the two drugs. That is when I decided to sell my ton of the Affy- type hash. I began selling it at two thousand dollars a pound and people couldn't get enough of it.

I had Rolf's money, all 6.4 million American dollars in ten duffle bags, delivered to New York Harbor by Pete's crew to the ship that had been dry-docked for a complete overhaul, including installation of a new diesel engine to replace the one that screwed up the one-hundred ton shipment. If this ship had been in excellent condition, I believe that the forty-four ton bust of the one ship would not have happened.

But for the reasons that weren't taken care of, all three ships would have made it safely into New York City Harbor and we would have been unloading 100 tons of hash instead of a paltry 22 tons, which would have made Rolf and I approximately 88 million dollars instead of the 6.5 million that was sent to him. However, Rolf was to make 80% of the 33 tons aboard the ship that landed safely in Montreal. The money from that hash deal would make Rolf about 11 million plus. Using three of Pete's money counting machines, it took eight days to count the money. So the total from the two ships averaged about eighteen million, not the 80 million that was expected.

I too had made a bundle of money and was now about to make even more selling the Afghani-type hash for one-thousand dollars or more, depending on the quantity sold.

I wired Rolf the problem we had with the three ships. I knew he was well aware of them and surmised that he wasn't too happy about the outcome. However, I was certain that he had made millions of dollars more than what he had paid for the hash, even though he lost the biggest shipment and wasn't certain regarding the outcome of the ship that had made it safely to Montreal. According to Pete, everything went well and Rolf received his money.

I also was in a state of ecstasy, making more money than ever before, and I didn't know what to do with it. I had well over six million, plus nearly a ton of the black Lebanese and a few boxes of different shades of the same hash that I had been turning into an Affy-looking hash, which I would sell for a great deal of money, depending upon the lack of hash in the market.

Cocaine was coming in by the tons, hash was practically non-existent. It was just a matter of time before the "dopers" would demand something to "smoke" so they could come down from the coke. That time was getting closer and closer. There was very little pot around and hash was just the thing to bring out to sell at one hundred pounds per week. Basically, I could sell the hash for just about any price I wanted.

I wasn't a greedy person, although I wanted to make up the money I had lost from the bust. Instead of splitting one hundred kilos, I had to split twenty two tons, which meant I lost about forty million dollars. However, the six million plus would suffice and I still had to sell the black hash, which would bring in another two to three million. I was sitting pretty. My only problem, besides selling the hash, was where to stash the boxes of money, hoping Pete's soldiers wouldn't steal it from me.

The following morning, I called Uncle Pete to make sure Rolf's money from me made it to its destination. He confirmed that it had. Pete, however, had something else on his mind and wanted me to meet him at his home to talk over a few "things," although he didn't mention what the "things" were.

Two hours later, I arrived at his place. His wife, as usual, opened the door and let me in. Also as usual, she left in a huff, saying she was leaving to visit her sisters. That was the usual procedure she went through when Pete had his friends visiting him for a "sit-down."

Pete greeted me as I entered his living room. Louie and Sal were sitting on a couch near the fireplace. Pete seemed to be in a jovial mood. Christmas was just a few days away and New Years was just around the corner. He invited me to his New Year's party to celebrate the coming of 1975.

"I'm sorry, Pete, I'm celebrating that night with my girlfriend."

"So, bring her along."

How could I refuse his request? I couldn't, and it was as simple as that. Partying with a houseful of "Goombas" wasn't my idea of a happy celebration. However, I had one problem: I had no girlfriend at that time. I would have to go alone.

#

Pete had me sit close to him in his favorite reclining chair, and had Sal pour everyone a glass of an expensive red wine from 1963. We toasted the coming New Year and then Pete sat near me on his couch, directly adjacent to the couch Sal and Louie were sitting in, and asked me why my girlfriend hadn't come along. I made the excuse that she wasn't feeling too well. Right away, he introduced me to a beautiful, dark-haired Italian girl named Maria. In fact, most girls there at the party were named Maria. We got along great the whole evening. She stuck to me like "glue." The party was a smash. However, I never did see Maria again after that night.

Pete was hoping Hoffa would show up for the celebration, but it never happened. He mentioned that Hoffa was getting old and didn't have the "toughness" he once had, since his lockup in the Federal Pen.

Pete was a Teamsters Union Delegate; one of his perks for being in the Detroit Mob and good friends with James Hoffa. It was a "no show" job, which meant he was paid a weekly paycheck and did not have to show up unless there was a problem between two locals that were vying for the same job.

After mentioning my concern about Rolf's money, as was agreed upon, I wanted to make sure the millions I had placed into Pete's hands had gotten to Rolf without any problems. Pete assured me the money was on its way to Amsterdam. I was satisfied with his answer, even though there was nothing more I could do other than believe Pete's words. As a precaution, I wired Rolf just to make sure he had received the money.

However, Pete seemed to be in another world concerning Rolf. He began talking about Jimmy Hoffa, his best and dear friend, who had been released from Federal Prison on December 23rd at 4:10 p.m. in 1971.

More than a week later, while Pete waited for Hoffa for a sit-down concerning his reinstatement as President of the Teamsters Union leader, I began selling my Lebanese hash over the next few months and made a "killing." People couldn't get enough of it for any price. Pot was unavailable and people wanted something to smoke during their cocaine parties.

I made more than two and a half million. The "Brotherhood of Love" returned and bought a ton of the black hash at one thousand dollars per pound. They actually believed it to be Afghani hash. The other few hundred pounds I sold between one thousand and two thousand dollars per pound within three months.

However, I had a major problem: where to stash the incredible amount of money. I was worried that Sal, Louie, or their associates would steal it and then whack me, so I came up with a solution. I rented a number of houses in four different cities, placed the money in aluminum trunks and buried them in the ground four feet deep in landscaped flower beds and allowed close friends to move in. I was certain the money would be safe. I just hoped Pete's soldiers wouldn't kidnap and torture me to hold me for ransom. I dreamt about that very circumstance nearly every night, many times waking up in a deep sweat. Many months went by before the nightmare disappeared. After all, it was only money.

When Hoffa was released from prison Pete told me he was as excited as his first day in school and he picked him up personally in a limousine. Fitzsimons had promised to pick him up on that special day, but never arrived. When the two met, Fitzsimons made excuse after excuse for not sending his limousine to pick Hoffa up personally, which Hoffa overlooked. Hoffa was outraged though, when he learned of the deal that was conceived between the Teamsters and the Nixon administration.

It seemed that Fitzsimons, who had become President of the Teamsters while Hoffa did his "time," had been consorting with the Nixon administration. If the Teamsters backed Nixon for his run for his second term as President, Nixon would pardon Hoffa, even though Hoffa had less than six months before his parole hearing came up for review; and Hoffa was sure he would be paroled. However, there was a hitch to the deal that Hoffa didn't know about. Hoffa, if pardoned, would have to forego his Union duties for a ten year period. Fitzsimons didn't mention this part of the agreement to his former Teamsters President because he knew Hoffa wouldn't have agreed to the deal. This came as a shock, when Hoffa learned about the deal to get him released from prison. Once he learned this, he became irate and wanted Fitzsimons dead.

Fitzsimons had the power and was under the control of the Mob. If Hoffa went against the Mob, his life wouldn't be worth a nickel. Fitzsimons had backstabbed Hoffa and Hoffa wanted revenge and his Presidency returned.

Because of this, Hoffa was a very disgruntled and angry man. He had taught Fitzsimons how to run the Teamsters during the 1930's and had then allowed him to control the Union until his release. That was the promise that the two had agreed upon. However, Fitzsimons didn't abide by the agreement…and Hoffa wasn't too happy with the situation. He made this known to Giacalone and the Underboss of the Mob.

Sometime in spring of 1975, Hoffa demanded a "sit-down" with the Underboss and demanded that Fitzsimons be "taken care of." However, his request was refused. Hoffa was outraged and told his friend of forty years that if "he wouldn't do him this favor, he would do what needed to be done himself." The Mob Underboss wasn't too happy with Hoffa's demands. In fact, Hoffa had disrespected the "Boss," which was a "No, No." However, he succumbed to Hoffa's demand and ordered the "sit-down" with the Mob entities who were the actual controller's of the Teamsters.

Fitzsimons was only a "lackey" for the Mob, even though he was the Teamsters President. The Detroit, Cleveland, and Gambino Mobs were the actual controllers of the International Brotherhood of Teamsters.

10
CHAPTER

The end of an era.

James R. Hoffa was having his problems with Fitzsimons, as he tried to get his old job back as President of the International Brotherhood of Teamsters. Hoffa was no longer able to trust the people whom he had made wealthy; associations that went back nearly forty years. I was having similar issues; no longer being able to trust friends whom I had known for nearly twenty years with the money I had entrusted them from the tons of hash I had sold. I was worried that one or more would dig gardens to raise vegetables and stumble onto the stash of money I had hidden there. Hoffa and I were similar in one respect—we were both paranoid about the people who surrounded us.

Pete suggested that I take approximately 90% of my earnings—more than two and a half million—from the hash deal and invest it with his outfit, earning me a ten percent profit. He told me he would invest the money in honest real estate deals. He promised to collect my profits and make sure my money was well looked out for and I wouldn't have to worry about my friends ripping me off.

The only problem I had now was how I would dig the money out of the ground without my friends realizing just how much money they were sitting on.

I did what Pete suggested, not without reservations, I may add, and had each of my friends dig into the ground where I told them. For their efforts, I gave them a few grand to keep their mouths shut. I delivered the money to Pete, using his money counters to count out the money. I gave him seven trunks full of cash and prayed that he would do me right.

After the money was counted, Pete got a phone call and by the look on his face he wasn't too happy. He hung up the phone and sat on his couch, a discouraged look on his face. He just stared without saying a word. He sat there for more than fifteen minutes, before he told us about the call. Sal, Louie, Pete, and I, with the OK from Giacalone, were to drive to New York and then New Jersey.

Pete was very quiet on this trip. He seemed "out of touch" with the people around him. Something was on his mind; something I hadn't seen in him before. He wasn't the boisterous self that he normally was, telling me how great things were for him and his "family." Now he was in "deep thought" for this complete trip and he barely said two words. I figured that he or one of his "Goombas" was going to do another hit. That's what I surmised, as I drove the 600 mile trip to NYC.

It was a relief when we finally arrived at our destination. Once again, we traveled to Mulberry Street to meet with Neil "Anyellow" Delecroche at the same place we had previously. Then I drove to the same bar that we had visited once before in New Jersey.

We parked in a space reserved just for us; everyone got out of the big Cadillac and slowly walked into the dimly lit bar. I thought we were there to see Corallo again; however, this time it was a different man, a rather large fellow. Even in the barely lit room, you could tell he had death written in his eyes: Someone else's death, not his.

THE AGE OF AQUARIUS II

Sal, Louie and I sat at the bar, while Pete had a sit-down with Neil and the new guy, whom I learned was the President of New Jersey's Teamsters Union, Tony Provozano. Even though he was a dominant figure in the New Jersey's Teamsters Union, he had Mob written all over his face.

Neil and Tony seemed to be in a better mood than Pete, ordering drink after drink, but Pete didn't drink a drop of his and seemed downright "pissed off."

I figured Pete had been given an "order" that he didn't agree with, because every now and then I would look over to their table and I could see that Pete, with head held low, was not agreeing with the other two gangsters and seemed to be pleading with them. Suddenly, Tony pounded his fist on the table top and pointed a finger at Pete, as if saying: You do as I say and that's it! This is what, I believe, Provozano was telling him. Pete just slumped in his seat, shook his head rather shamefully and took his orders like the soldier he was. And that was the end of it.

After that incident, they all ordered drinks and drank to celebrate the "turn of events."

Ten minutes after the three Mobsters had downed a number of drinks, Pete shouted to Sal, Louie, and me that it was "time to leave." I left to start the Caddy and waited for the gangsters. I had no idea of what was to come. I just drove the car and kept my mouth shut, unless called upon for my opinion to a question.

I noticed Delecroche stayed behind and it was just me, Sal, Louie, and Pete. As they all shuffled into the car, Pete yelled to me, "Let's get the fuck out of here and fast. We gotta get back to Detroit as fast as we can. I need to speak with Giacalone about this sit-down." And that was about all he had to say throughout the ride back to Allen Park: Just as he had during our ride to NY City.

I sensed something didn't go too well for Pete at the sit-down. He just looked out his side window for hours, thinking, not saying a word. I wondered what the hell had happened at that sit-down to make Pete act the way he was. After a few hours of silence, Pete lay back and slept for a few hours. He awoke when we stopped in Pennsylvania for gasoline. Once we were back on the road, he again fell asleep, as if he wanted to just disappear. I had never seen him like this until this trip. He always seemed on "top of the world" and that nobody could hurt or destroy him. He wasn't his usual jovial self, that was for sure.

About ten hours after leaving New Jersey, we arrived at Pete's house. As I pulled into his driveway, he yelled at Sal and Louie, "Get the FUCK out of the car and I'll call you when I need you…which may be soon."

That was it. We all got out of the car and headed in separate directions. All the way to my place, I wondered what Pete had gotten himself into.

11
CHAPTER

Hoffa Whacked: Mobsters after me: Returned to Afghanistan.

A few weeks later, Pete called and told me to meet him at his house within the hour. Seeing that I had invested most of my earnings from the hash deal into legitimate businesses that the Mob backed, I did as I was told. I was at his house five minutes earlier than ordered.

Pete met me at the door and handed me his car keys. "Let's drive, kid," he said.

While driving to a favorite gangster eating facility, The Red Fox Inn, I found out the reason why he wasn't himself during our escapade during our long drive to New Jersey and back. It was what the gentlemen in question wanted Pete to do if Jimmy Hoffa decided to run for re-election for the President of the Teamsters.

As I was driving Pete's new Caddy to the restaurant, Pete, all of a sudden, burdened with a heavy load, blurted out that the Gambino and Colombo Families wanted things to stay as they were because they had Fitzsimons in their pocket and he was a "pussy" compared to Hoffa. Fitzsimons was also a good friend to the "White House."

Hoffa was a leader and when he was president of the Teamsters, he gave orders to the Mob, whereas the Mob controlled Fitzsimons and they wanted it to stay that way. They believed Hoffa would have too much "Government heat" on him, twenty-four hours a day, 365 days a year.

Therefore, the two strongest Mobs in New York wanted Pete to do the job for them, because he was a neighbor and good friend of Hoffa. Pete actually refused his orders, but then reconsidered the consequences if he didn't do the "hit."

Pete went on to tell me that Provozano believed Pete could convince Hoffa to ride with him for lunch or dinner and then, before or after, kill him. They would do the rest.

Pete was to drive a new Caddy (that would be delivered to his house on that particular day) and after the "hit," with Hoffa in it, drop it off at a junk yard to be squished into a 2ft. square. It would then be taken to an Armenian-owned foundry in Detroit, where car and body would be smelted at a temperature of around 3500 degrees. Hoffa's body would be evaporated within a few minutes, leaving no evidence.

I remember Pete telling me it was to be taken to A&L Salvage or S&L Salvage and Junk Yard and the "people that gave the order" would see to it that he got home safe and sound.

Pete knew, however, that if he did do the "hit," one of two things could happen on his return trip home: His own soldiers would whack him, so there would be no one left to "rat" out La Cosa Nostra, or he would get home safely. The possibility of being left unscathed, Pete believed, was not a possibility.

After listening to his situation, I was hoping he wouldn't go through with the job. However, he was the "Capo and soldier" and had to follow orders. The possibility of being dumped into the Detroit River—alive and wearing concrete boots or with a bullet behind the ear—was part of the sacrifice a "made man" had to deal with. Pete was definitely in a precarious situation and I wanted nothing to do with it.

It was only a few months before the election and Hoffa was the favorite. Fitzsimons didn't have the "balls" to stop him from running for re-election; however, the Mob would do whatever was necessary to turn the "heat" away from the Teamsters.

The Feds would make it their number one priority to stop Hoffa from returning to one of the largest Unions built. It was the papers he had signed (without his knowledge, of course) for his pardon that stated that the Feds had the right to stop him from running. They took their time, with all their bureaucracy crap, so Hoffa wouldn't be able to get his appeal about the wording of his pardon in front of the Appellate Court in time for the election.

Evidently, Hoffa was disgusted with the whole situation and just said "Fuck it." Hoffa believed he had made the Teamsters Union, with all his hard work and diligence, as big as it was and that he believed it was his "right" to again be the President of that Union. In fact, before entering the Federal Prison, Hoffa explicitly told Fitzsimons that he could be President until he was released from Prison.

Hoffa had a right to be angry. Fitzsimons had screwed him, along with Nixon's partners in crime, Charles Coleson and the Don of the Detroit Mafia.

Even so, a few days after Nixon's resignation, Hoffa, along with the hierarchy of the Union and a few of the hierarchy of the Detroit Mob had a big party to celebrate. Words were exchanged during the party which led Hoffa to believe that he had gotten the OK from those who were now in control. However, Hoffa didn't hear what he had thought he had heard.

The "bosses" figured, with Ford as President, that nothing had changed, since Fitzsimons had had meetings with the new President and had golfed with him.

During this time, Hoffa believed that his pardon contract was now null and void, since all of the people involved with his pardon were now Felons themselves and many now stashed away in the same Federal Prison where Hoffa had served his sentence. However, that wasn't the case.

Fitzsimons wasn't about to let go of his job that easily. He had the power and Hoffa didn't. Hoffa took it upon himself, along with his many attorneys, to once again deal with the legal system that had sent Hoffa "up the river."

Our Governmental system again slowed, as it wanted nothing to do with wiping away the few words of Hoffa's pardon that were so important to him. Those few words stated, "Hoffa may not be in or around any Union organizations for ten years from his release from Federal prison." That meant that he had another six years before he could run for President of the Teamsters. Hoffa, being seventy-five years of age, was nothing more than a "has-been" as far as the Teamster hierarchy was concerned.

Hoffa, to say the least, was outraged. He overstepped his bounds when he threatened his Mob friends that he was going to get rid of Fitzsimmons if it "killed him." Evidently, his premonition came true.

Pete once again phoned me, saying he wanted to speak with me about a "life or death" situation. Those words made me very nervous and frightened. I knew he wanted to talk with me about the Hoffa "hit."

I was right. My premonition was "right on."

Once I arrived at Pete's place, he told me the "hit" was on and that he had been given the job. I could tell he was very paranoid. All the shades were pulled down, sweat was pouring off his face and he wasn't the "confident" Pete I usually knew. This job was eating his guts. He seemed to be more nervous than I was. Then he said the words I didn't want to hear.

"I want YOU to drive me and Hoffa to the Red Fox Inn. But just for a 'sit-down' with the 'powers that be,' to try one last time to change their minds."

THE AGE OF AQUARIUS II

I didn't know who he was talking about—Fitzsimmons, the Mob, whomever; I didn't care who it was. I wanted nothing to do with it. I got the idea that if Hoffa refused their request, he would not be seen again.

Pete told me to be at his house around 2 p.m., in two days. With that said, I drove back to my place. I had had enough. I wanted nothing more to do with him or the Mob, and now I had less than two days to figure a way out of this predicament I had gotten myself into.

My words came back to haunt me. Once the Mob does you a favor, you feel obligated to them or it would be your time to die. Hell, I was only twenty-five years old and wasn't ready to have my body cut into little pieces, then fed to hungry hogs. I definitely wasn't ready to die. Not that way, anyway. I felt when it was my time to leave this world for another, the Supreme Being above would take care of that.

Being Pete's part-time driver and was seen driving Pete and Hoffa to their favorite restaurant, I didn't want anyone to get the idea that I was involved in the "job" Pete was ordered to do.

I decided to leave town and return to Afghanistan, the country that had kicked me out. However, I stayed until 1976.

#

I wanted to see the outcome of Pete's actions. I hadn't seen him since the day I had dropped him off at home after driving him to New Jersey for his sit-down with the "bosses," just a few weeks before that fateful day.

I remember that day. Hoffa was last seen leaving that restaurant around mid-afternoon on July 30th, 1975.

Watching and listening to many TV stations, Pete's name wasn't brought up. Chucky O'Brian was the only name mentioned. According to the FBI, he was the main suspect, along with suspected Mob members.

I wanted to find out what had happened to Pete, so I had my mother phone his wife and ask her how he was doing.

I learned that he had gotten into a near fatal head-on collision with a Teamster's semi. Nearly every bone in his body had been broken. While at the hospital, his heart had stopped beating twice and he was brought back to life, but then fell into a coma for five days and was put on a ventilator.

A month later, Pete had come out of his coma and had gotten some of his strength back and he began talking. He told his wife that he went to have a secret meeting with a few members of his crew in a farmer's cornfield and they turned on him and beat him with baseball bats. Thinking he was dead, they placed him into his Cadillac on a deserted road, where he had the head-on collision.

Pete, the stubborn man that he was, had withstood the beating and crash and was taken to the hospital by the owner of the farm.

I decided to fly back to the country that I had nearly died in: Afghanistan. I knew I was taking a chance, but my life was on the line so I had to try.

My passport still had those words written in Dari that stated I was a "spy" and not allowed to return to their country. I was hoping, though, that Afghan customs wouldn't see that particular page and if they did, I figured I could give them enough "baksheesh" (bribe) so they would allow me to enter their country once again.

With that thinking in mind, I left behind everything I had worked so hard for; all the millions of dollars Pete had invested for me into his "supposedly" legitimate operations. If Pete got whacked for doing the Hoffa hit, I wouldn't see a dime of that money anyway.

I quickly put together a couple of grand, a one-way plane ticket to Kabul, Afghanistan, via Gatwick Airport in England, and threw a few clothes into my handmade backpack/coat along with my Polaroid camera. That was it. This time, I knew I wasn't returning to America.

Even though I was on a methadone program, taking one-hundred milligrams of liquid methadone a day due to my morphine habit, I took the chance anyway; even though I knew I would go through withdrawals during my long trip.

I received my last dose a few hours before leaving for the airport. I hoped it would last until I reached Kabul.

Unfortunately, that wasn't to be. As soon as I reached Gatwick Airport, I was in need for another dose of methadone. I asked a "Bobbie" where the airport doctor's office was. Even though it was Sunday, I knew they had an Airport Doctor from the experience in 1967, when we met Arlene Shwablene's father who was the doctor for Kennedy Airport. I was right. The officer pointed to the doctor's building just a short hop from the main gates. It took me all of five minutes to reach it.

When I reached the doctor's office, I introduced myself to the only nurse on duty that day and explained my problem to her. She was very understanding, but not before she mentioned that I "should return to America" and get help there. I then lied to her that I was going to New Delhi, India to Connaught Circle for rehab treatment. Just as I finished my story, the doctor came into the office. The nurse then explained my situation to him. He parroted the same words to me that the nurse had: Return to America for help.

I explained to the doctor that I did not plan to return to America and asked him for a hundred milligram dose of methadone. He stated that he didn't have that type of drug in his office and if he could get it, he would have to go into London and hope that he could get it there, being Sunday and all. I begged him and told him it was his job to help me. I could tell those words hit deep in his heart. When he heard my name was Willingham, he mentioned something about the Willinghams being related to the Queen.

I kept silent about that and begged him again to "help me" and that my plane to India was leaving within a few hours. The nurse then asked to see my ticket. Damn, I thought, I'm busted. She saw that the ticket was for Afghanistan, not India, and told me that she could have it changed with no problem.

I refused her offer and lied through my teeth once again, telling her that the ticket agency had given me that ticket and said it was for India and I adamantly stated that fact, over and over. She knew I was lying and so did the doctor. He, however, was on my side and told his nurse, "If that's what he wants to do, we can't do anything about it."

I also told the two that I had a very bad toothache along with my withdrawal problem. They were very friendly and sympathetic to my needs. The doctor said that he would have to hurry to the druggist in hopes of getting the methadone that I needed. With that said, he left in a hurry. The nurse had me sit in a chair and took one pill out of a bottle and held it on the wisdom tooth that was giving me such a problem. She held it there for more than three minutes, until it had dissolved and made my tooth numb. I thanked her and then suddenly fell asleep. I awoke about ten minutes before the doctor arrived.

The nurse came into the room and saw that I had awakened and said, "You fell asleep for more than two hours. How are you feeling?"

"My tooth doesn't hurt anymore. That pill really helped me. Thank you. Has the doctor returned yet?"

"No," she retorted, "but he should be here very shortly."

"I hope he got my methadone."

"I still say you should return to your country."

"I hate our Government. It's the most corrupt Government in the world. Every politician is a crook," I babbled.

"We have the same problem here, honey."

Ten minutes after our discussion, the doctor returned with a smile on his face and sweating profusely. He had been gone for nearly three hours and I had about forty minutes to make my flight.

"I couldn't find any druggists open, so I had to go to a hospital to get this," he said as he handed me four tablets—each one containing ten milligrams of methadone—and a glass of water. He added, "I couldn't find any liquid methadone, so those will have to hold you until you get to India."

THE AGE OF AQUARIUS II

I presumed it was methadone. Hell, it could have been sugar pills. However, I was in no position to question his integrity. He seemed to be a trustful doctor and someone who took his Hippocratic Oath seriously.

I thanked him and his nurse for helping me. They were both in their later years of life and treated me as a "son."

A few minutes later, I was walking back to the main building to catch my flight to Kabul. Once I had gone through security checks, I had only twenty minutes before boarding time.

By the time we began boarding the plane, the pills had kicked in and I felt much, much better. I just prayed that it was enough to hold me until I arrived at Kabul and could buy some opium to take care of my addiction problem.

During the flight, a girl directly across the aisle had some liqueur she had bought in Greece and asked the people around her if they wanted a "swig." I didn't like alcohol, but I was coming down fast from my methadone and took a big swig from the bottle and passed it back to her.

I had also brought with me a number of hash joints rolled in tobacco, which I hoped would cover up the Afghani hash smell. I had smoked one during the flight without any problems. And after asking the girl with the liqueur for another swig, she reluctantly obliged. We were flying over Afghanistan, nearing Kabul, when I decided to smoke my last hash joint. That turned out to be a BIG mistake. Nearing the end of finishing the joint, a male steward walked by and could smell hash smoke in the air. I had just put the joint out and smashed it in the ashtray, with the rolled up cardboard filter still in it. The Afghan steward flew into an outrage.

Looking directly at me, he asked to see my cigarettes. "Hashish! Hashish!" he bellowed for all to hear.

Luckily, I only had a few cigarettes left in the pack, but no hash joints. I had already smoked them during our long twelve hour flight.

He viciously tore open the pack, as if he was a law enforcement officer, but didn't find any incriminating evidence. However, he did take the ashtray with him to the back of the plane and said something to the other stewardesses. I turned my head so I could see "what was going down" and the Steward dumped the ashes and butts onto a white piece of paper. I knew that was a "bad omen."

I was worried enough about the words in my passport when I was deported just two years before. Now I was worried that he would phone ahead to customs and tell them of this situation.

Thirty minutes later, we were on the ground, landing safely at Kabul. I gathered what little baggage I had and had my passport and tax money inside my passport ready for customs. I put the tax money, ten Afghani, about twenty-five cents in a place that wasn't anywhere near the words written against me, hoping customs would grab the money, look at my picture and visa and allow me to enter their beautiful country. Unfortunately, that wasn't the case. I watched as the customs man went through every page and read the words written by a communist Afghan. I tried to bribe my way in. That didn't work. I didn't use Mr. Barrack's name because I didn't want to get him into any trouble. Now that I think back, I should have. He most likely could have calmed things down and the customs man would have let me enter their country.

Instead, I was placed under house arrest. Three soldiers were to stay with me until the following day.

I asked, "What then?"

Instead of an answer, all I got was the barrel of a rifle buried into the middle of my back, moving me forward.

After leaving the airport, the three soldiers placed me into a truck, the same type used when I was caught years before trying to smuggle myself out of the country, which took me from the Eastern Afghan border to a dark dungeon. This time, though, I was taken to a familiar place: A restaurant that was near Tiar's home. Tiar was one of two dear friends from whom I had bought my hash, hash oil and opium. Why they chose that place I had no idea.

However, before going to the restaurant, I had the taxi driver stop at the "Devil's" Pharmacy where, for four years, I had bought my pharmaceutical morphine.

Using a twenty Afghani bill I bribed the lead soldier to allow me to visit the pharmacy. He took it, with no questions asked.

As I hopped out of the truck, so did the soldier I had bribed and he stood lookout with his rifle at the ready, just in case I tried to escape. I had no plans of escaping. All I wanted was morphine to stop my withdrawal symptoms. I told the soldiers to wait outside while I went inside to visit my old friend.

As soon as I entered the pharmacy, the Devil remembered me and smiled; that is, until he saw the soldiers and their rifles. Suddenly, I was no longer a friend, but a threat to him and his illegal business. He quickly threw me out; I left empty-handed. I understood his reasoning as he could have been executed if he was caught selling morphine illegally.

The soldiers and I got back into the truck and drove to an undisclosed location. I thought I was going to be thrown once again into a cold, dirty, and dark dungeon.

Instead, they drove to the restaurant.

After one of the soldiers spoke with the owner, I was taken upstairs to a large bedroom with four beds. The leader of the three soldiers pointed to a bed that I was to use. He quickly spoke to the other two soldiers and once the conversation was over, the two men left the room and didn't return.

I tried to make friends with the soldier, but he wanted nothing to do with me. That is, until I began speaking to him in Farsi and explained my situation to the best of my ability. Remember, it had been two years since I had been thrown out of the country and my Farsi was a little rusty.

Within a fifteen minute period, he had changed his tune about me and saw that I wasn't a threat. I bought us each tea and kabob. At first, he declined the food and drink. Then, a small boy of twelve came into the room and I spoke with him in English and explained to him why I was in Afghanistan and what had happened two years earlier. He then explained this to the soldier. That put the man at ease and took me up on my offer to share dinner with me. Afterwards, I showed him my passport and the words written in it and told him it "wasn't true" and that I was only "a tourist who had overstayed my visa."

I asked the boy if he knew of a person named Tiar. To my surprise, he did. I gave him fifty Afghani to bring him to the restaurant. Within minutes, my old friend arrived. When he saw me and the soldier guarding me, he seemed very nervous and acted as though he didn't know me, and I considered him to be one of my best friends. I used to visit with him, his wife, and kids at his home, which was now forbidden. I couldn't understand it. Even so, I talked him into sitting with me and to have some tea. He obliged my request. The soldier did not.

During our conversation, Tiar told me things about what was happening to his country and how he could be killed just for talking to a foreigner. I couldn't believe this was the same Afghanistan that I had left more than two years earlier. It had turned Communist and the Government was executing Afghan citizens for inexcusable reasons that made no sense: Like talking with me for instance. Tiar also told me that it was impossible for him to travel to the places where he once bought his hash powder and opium. He further explained how the Afghan government was spying on their own people and we were being spied upon as we spoke. That was the reason he was so paranoid. I couldn't believe this. Within five minutes, after he had finished his tea, he was gone…disappearing into the night.

What a change in governmental policies, I thought to myself.

Foreigners also were not allowed to travel within the country without a government official traveling with them.

THE AGE OF AQUARIUS II

After Tiar left, the soldier and I returned to my room. My withdrawals were beginning to get worse and I began getting muscle spasms, which my new friend seemed afraid of. He thought I was sick and was concerned that he would catch whatever it was that I had. When the boy came to pick up our cups and saucers, I asked him if he could get me some Opium or in Farsi called, "Teriot" (pronounced Tear-e-ot) (such as tear up some paper).

I thought the soldier would be angry with me; however, after the boy explained my problem to him. I promised the boy one-hundred Afghani if he would get me a chunk of the black tarry substance to relieve me of my withdrawal symptoms. I asked the soldier if he wanted some and he shook his head "yes," but with "Chi," which meant: tea.

We both smiled and within a few minutes the boy came up with two small paper packets which the opium was wrapped in. The boy gave me the packet, so I picked out the biggest piece of the two and gave the other to the soldier. The boy then gave us each another cup of tea to help the opium dissolve and go down easier. With that done, I gave the boy three American dollars, which was closer to one–hundred-and-fifty Afghani than one hundred. Each dollar was worth forty-eight Afghani, the same as it was worth when I had left more than two years before.

Within fifteen minutes, my muscle spasms were gone and, ten minutes later, I was fast asleep.

We were awakened by the singing of the Imam from the tower of the largest Mosque in Kabul. After my new friend had prayed, we went downstairs to the restaurant and sat at one of the tables. I ordered each of us tea and "Teriot." However, this time the soldier refused the little piece of opium, so I ate both pieces and swallowed it down with a sip of tea.

Within ten minutes, after I had finished my tea, I felt the opium tingle throughout my body. Not like the rush from shooting the morphine. It was just strong enough to stop my aching body from the muscle spasms. Just as we finished our tea, a large military truck pulled up to the curb in front of the doors of the restaurant and a dozen soldiers, with rifles in hand, jumped out from the back of it. The top officer, a captain, came into the restaurant and as soon as my soldier saw him, he motioned me to stand up, pointed his rifle at me, and pointed towards the open door.

I wasn't handcuffed or ruffed up. My guard told his captain that I "wasn't a threat." That said, I was taken to the truck and lifted to the back of it and sat on a wooden plank near the cab, while the dozen guards sat near me on both sides, with rifles at the ready. My guard and his captain sat in the front seat along with the driver.

I had no idea what was to happen to me. Would I be sent to jail? Would I be shot? I was uncertain of the complexity of my crime. I thought for sure I would be taken in front of the same Judge who had heard my case two years before, when Mr.B. saved my butt from the hangman's noose or the executioner who beheaded people for crimes similar to mine. I was literally shaking.

As the three soldiers in the front seat were speaking amongst themselves, one turned to me, took his index finger, and slid it across the front of his neck, as though he was telling me my throat would be slit. However, my new friend just laughed and shook his head, "no," then said in perfect English, "Don't be worried. My friends don't like Americans and want all Americans dead."

Oh Great, I thought to myself. They're gonna kill me. Shaking his head "no" didn't help my situation at all. Even so, I thanked him for his words. However, I didn't believe him, even when he told me that I'd be placed onto a plane and sent to another country. He said they would allow me to choose the country of choice. I picked India, but it wasn't New Delhi; it was the border city of Amritsar. I had no idea why they had picked that city. I found it hard to believe that I would leave Afghanistan unharmed.

THE AGE OF AQUARIUS II

As I waited to see what would happen next, Tiar's words swirled inside my head, especially about foreigners not being allowed to travel without a government escort.

When the King was in power, foreigners were allowed to travel anywhere in the country **without** an escort. The only province you couldn't go alone was Nuristan, which was a smuggling point for opium and weapons.

I wondered why Moktar and his Mujahedeen allowed this to happen. I was certain he and his fellow "freedom fighters" were against the new President and his Russian comrades. I explicitly remember him telling me, "Bob, we are Freedom Fighters, Mujahedeen. When the people don't like the government, we fight that government."

Where were they now? I thought to myself.

I believed an all out civil war would come soon. A few years later, my premonition came true.

Mohammad Daoud, the King's cousin, who once was the Prime Minister, had control over the military during his reign and when the King flew to England for eye surgery, Daoud phoned the top Generals of the Army, who he had given them their rank and power, made a few phone calls, and told them that he was now President of the country and brought the Russians to Afghanistan. Unfortunately for him, however, that was his downfall. In 1978, just five years after the coup that put him in power, he refused an order from the highest ranking Russian and they assassinated him. The Russians then placed their own man as President and within a year they assassinated him. Two other puppet Presidents for the Russians also met their downfall this way. That is what started the Afghan-Soviet Union war.

A "Fatwa" was ordered by the head Mullah or Imam (Priest) which ordered all Afghans to fight a holy war against the invading Soviet Union Military, to stand up to their aggression against the Afghan people. Even the Afghan children took up arms to fight the invaders. It was twenty-five million Afghans against one hundred thousand Russians. Every invading country that tried to take control of the Afghanistan people lost "big time."

It took ten years of fighting before the Mighty Russian Army turned tail and ran back to their homeland. It was a joyous day for the mighty Afghans, especially the "Mujahedeen," the "Freedom Fighters."

It was a great victory, until the Afghans began fighting each other: Province against Province, tribe against tribe.

The Mujahedeen, however, stood to the side, awaiting a new government and President.

Saudi Arabia funneled money to the Pakistani Intelligence Service who, in turn, funneled the money to the Afghani's, who backed the Wahhabists, who were taught thirty years before by the Saudi Mullahs. They had enough money to buy the Mujahedeen to help defeat the so-called warlords and their soldiers, one province at a time. They fought for a political party of right-wingers who believed in strict Sharia Law, called the "Taliban."

Fighting for the "Taliban Party" was the biggest mistake the Mujahedeen could have made, in my opinion. The Taliban stood for everything the Mujahedeen was against. The Mujahedeen loved music, flying kites, smoking hashish, and eating or smoking opium. These were their only vices that I knew of. They believed in most of the other Taliban laws, including Sharia law, which has been in existence since Afghanistan became a country in 1747, when Ahmad Durrani brought all the tribes together. He was known as "the father of Afghanistan."

Before then, Persia had control of that part of the world. The Indian Moguls controlled the Southern part, which was made up of today's Pakistan and India, while the Pashtu's held the ground they live on to this day. In 1921, King Amanullah signed the Treaty of Rawalpindi, which gave the Afghans their Independence.

I hoped the powers that be would give me back my independence.

THE AGE OF AQUARIUS II

In the ten minutes it took us to get to our destination, my paranoia kicked in. I believed I was about to be thrown into that same dark and dirty dungeon I had been placed into more than two years before.

I thought about mentioning the name of my friend and high government official, Mr. Barrack, then thought against it. I again believed if I mentioned his name and they thought he was a friend of mine in this new communist type government, his life and job most likely would be in jeopardy. I bit my tongue and waited until I saw what was going to happen to me.

We slowly filed out of the truck. I was then surrounded by my guards and taken into the same judicial building I had been in the last time I had visited Afghanistan. This time, however, I wasn't thrown into jail. Instead, I was taken to a large room with a large table. Sitting behind it were three, I assumed, government officials because they weren't garbed in the usual military clothes, but rather expensive western suits. My passport, opened to the page in question, was sitting on the table in front of them.

A very large, fat man, sitting in the middle of the three men, told me, in English, to "sit down" in a chair, three feet across from them and directly in front of the fat man.

"Why are you here?" the fat man asked.

"I returned to Kabul to visit my Afghan friends, whom I haven't seen or heard from in over two years."

"And what friends are these?" asked the short and skinny man to my left.

"The people I had known when I lived here."

"And who might that be? Give me some names," asked the man to my right. He appeared to be the youngest of the three, about my age—twenty-five.

"What does it matter? If you must know, I saw one of my friends last night at the restaurant your government had me stay at, along with an armed guard."

All three men spoke perfect English, which meant that they were most likely educated men, surmising that they worked for the Afghan government. I just wasn't sure if they were from customs, intelligence agents, or even possibly Americans working for the American Embassy.

"You mean you weren't taken to jail after being questioned by the customs agent at the airport?" asked the fat man.

When I told them "no," all three seemed very surprised. "Why would they take me to jail when I didn't do anything? I'm here as a tourist."

The fat man suddenly stood up, somewhat upset and frustrated with my answers. "But your passport states that you spied for the American Government."

"That's a lie. I overstayed my visa because I loved your country and people and wanted to live here forever. I was angry with my government and their war against Vietnam." I added, "The American government and politicians are the most corrupt in the world."

The three nodded in unison. The fat man then replied, "Yes it is. But why should we believe you?"

"I'm telling the truth, that's why. Allah knows I'm speaking the truth."

When I mentioned "Allah" the young man seemed to become angry. His face suddenly turned red and looked angrily into my eyes in a way that made me nervous and edgy.

"How dare you mention Allah? You are not Muslim. You are an infidel," he said for all to hear, giving me a dirty look.

The fat man calmed the young man down, patting him on the back and slightly pushed him into his chair.

"Tell us the truth and we will be lenient with you. You returned to Kabul to spy for your country. Don't be afraid. You can tell us. We will not harm you. Admit it and you can leave Kabul without any repercussions," said the fat man, smiling.

"No! I told you, I am not a spy. I am just a tourist," I declared, slapping my hand on the table. That startled the three men, especially the fat man.

THE AGE OF AQUARIUS II

I remembered saying those same words just two years earlier when I was nearly killed while trying to smuggle myself out of Afghanistan and into Pakistan. Afghan soldiers killed my driver, shooting him in the side of the head as he knelt on a rock-covered road.

After my driver had been pulled out of the car and I, from the trunk, I had been told to kneel down. I was surrounded by a dozen or so soldiers, when suddenly one of their rifles supposedly misfired, splattering my friend's brains and skin all over the side of my face. As he slowly fell forward, dying, I could see his hand spasm, until one of the soldiers kicked him over to make sure he was dead. I was in shock. I thought my turn was next and pleaded for mercy.

The soldiers' superior had come out of a small building to see what all the commotion was about and saw the dead man lying in a pool of blood. He then ordered his men to drive me to Kabul (after being questioned and told I was spying for the American Infidels.)

I was soon thrown into the back of a military truck, guarded by a dozen soldiers. During the three hour ride, silence flooded the truck. I was still in shock from my friend's killing and the soldiers just stared at me, saying nothing. That was a time I wanted to forget.

After a two hour talk with these three, I believe, judges, I was told to wait out in the corridor and would be called back in for their answer concerning my punishment.

Punishment, I thought? The day before I was told I was to be flown to Amritsar, India sometime today.

My thoughts were driving me crazy. I thought only about my execution, never a thought about leaving Kabul alive.

Finally, my judgment was executed. The most outspoken mediator, judge, or whoever he was told me I was extremely lucky to be given a lenient sentence.

I figured his words meant that I was to be sent to jail for a period of time; however, I was mistaken.

I was told they declined a number of choices to which was in their power to hand down. One was fifty lashes with a whip, a 3 year jail sentence, or to be sent to another country, never to be allowed to visit their country again—forever. I was to be sent to the designated country that was first mentioned to me. India: Amritsar, India, which bordered the southern part of Pakistan near the city of Lahore. I was to be put on a plane within two hours.

I thanked them and was then ushered out of the room guarded by three armed soldiers and taken by truck to Kabul airport.

While waiting for my plane, my dear friend, Mr. Barrack, found me sitting amongst the three armed guards. After speaking with the soldiers, Mr. B. was allowed to sit with me while the guards stood on the other side of the room. He was very happy to see me and asked, "Why didn't you mention my name to the customs people as soon as you entered the country. I could have gotten you out of this mess."

I respectfully thanked him for his concern and said, "I thought I might have gotten you into trouble and didn't know if you wanted to see me because I never answered your last letter when you visited America."

I explained to him that our phone calls were intercepted by my government, the FBI, and I had been told not to contact him again. He said he understood, but at the time was very unhappy and worried because I did not contact him. Again I explained that it was out of my hands and that I would have been thrown in jail if I had kept up a correspondence with him. Either his government or mine didn't want us communicating.

I told him that I would keep in touch with him, if and when I returned to America. He asked why I would not return to America and I made it very clear that I didn't care for our corrupt justice system. He also had the same insight of my government and his.

We also believed that all governments and politicians were corrupt and not good people. Mr. B. and I talked for nearly thirty minutes before the soldiers returned and after we said our "goodbyes." I was taken into a small room, searched, and ordered to wait until I was ready to board my plane to India. I was then handed a ticket and walked through customs to a bus that took me and other people to our plane.

Within twenty minutes, I was off into the "Wild Blue Yonder." The plane ride lasted only thirty minutes. We landed at the border town of Amritsar, a city controlled by the Sikhs (pronounced: Seeks), a very prosperous and proud people who believed in never cutting their hair or beards and who were becoming known politically for their fundamentalist views against their government. They believed the Hindu Government was ignoring the importance of their tribe, which caused many arguments and incited radicalism within their ranks. They expected the Government to show them some "respect" and to allow them their own independence and their own province and lands. However, the Government refused their demands, so the Sikhs began gathering weapons and bomb making materials to show the Government that they "meant business." They figured if words didn't work, maybe bombs might get the Government's attention.

Other than that, the city of Amritsar was known for the "Golden Temple," a temple that was carved out of marble and gold. Behind the temple was a small oval wading pool. According to legend, a mother had carried her small deformed daughter to visit a tribal priest in a town nearby. However, she had become tired after carrying her child nearly twenty miles and she had to stop at the pond to quench their thirst. While the mother was wetting a dry rag to wipe her daughter's forehead to cool her down, she noticed her daughter crawling towards the pond. The mother leaped to her feet so her daughter wouldn't fall into the water and drown, but before the mother could reach her, her precious daughter dipped her index finger of her right hand into the pond and miraculously her deformities disappeared instantly. To say the least, everyone around or near her couldn't believe their eyes and praised

Buddha for making this girl "whole" again. From that day forward, the name of the building and pond was called "The Golden Temple."

To this day, people from all over the world come to this temple and are continuously hoping for their loved ones that the diseases that plague them will disappear. Faith is their best hope. To this day, the sick who go there claim their illnesses disappear.

Going through customs, as when I went through customs in New Delhi two years previously, my bags and my person weren't searched. I went through without a problem. Again, my bags could have been packed with kilos of hashish or illicit drugs and I wouldn't have had a problem.

Even though I was not allowed to visit Afghanistan, I was happy to be in India and especially Amritsar.

The first thing I did, once I flagged down a taxi, was to ask the cab driver if he knew where I could buy some opium. Within five minutes, I was able to buy approximately five grams of the drug. However, it wasn't as potent as the Affy opium, so I went to the poorer part of the city and began asking for morphine.

Soon, I met a doctor who had a small office and was able to purchase a hundred gram ampoule of liquid morphine. I also purchased a syringe from him and he then directed me to a small part of the room that had a single bed. I placed the needle into the ampoule and sucked all of it into the syringe. I shot all of it into my vein and within thirty seconds I was laying on the bed while the rush of the drug went through my body. A minute later, I felt like a new person. However, it wasn't as good as the half-grain tablets I had been used to, but it sufficed.

I paid the doctor ten rupees, which was a dollar in American money, thanked him, and was on my way to find a place to rest my body.

I found a cheap, but clean, room and decided to go to Srinagar, Kashmir to find some of that great Kashmiri hash.

THE AGE OF AQUARIUS II

Early the next morning, I bought a bus ticket and was on my way to the "Land of OZ," as the dope heads called it. However, after nearly a ten hour bus ride, which took me about ten thousand feet above sea level, I felt my energy dissipate, as my morphine no longer had an effect on my body.

I asked a few orange-haired hippies where I could buy some morphine or opium and was told that there was none to be had. They told me to go to Pakistan to buy the morphine that I had used for four years while I lived in Kabul. I immediately left my hotel room, even before I unpacked my bags, and set out to return to Amritsar. From there, it was a hop, skip and jump to the border of Pakistan.

When I reached the border of Pakistan, I was given a happy greeting from the customs official and a twenty-one day transit visa.

Within an hour, I was in Lahore, found some orange-haired European hippies who directed me to the pharmacy that sold the drug I needed. I bought ten bottles of the same half-grain tablets, which held twenty tablets of pure morphine that I had bought in Afghanistan. I was delighted.

After finding a cheap hotel room, I used my syringe I had purchased in Amritsar and injected three half-grain tablets, which knocked me back on my bed and I felt the ecstasy that I hadn't felt in more than two years. It brought back some great memories. I was on "top of the world."

I stayed in Lahore for just a few days, before leaving for Islamabad.

My plan was to go to Peshawar, which was just a few kilometers from the Afghan border, get an Afghan visa, and hope customs wouldn't find the synopsis of spying for the USA in my passport, and then travel by bus to Kabul and if need be, use my ticket to return to my homeland.

It sounded easy. However, nothing was easy for me. My luck was always "BAD."

Just before boarding a train to Islamabad, I met another American named Tommy who had no money or drugs and no place to rest his weary head. I felt sorry for him and asked if he wanted to join me and I would help him as best I could. He immediately took me up on my offer.

I paid for both our tickets and bought each of us a kabob sandwich. I figured I had enough money for both of us for a few days. I didn't know he had become my adopted brother. I paid for everything: drugs, food, and a hotel room. After a few days of this, he started getting on my nerves. He had quite a morphine habit and thought he could use me. However, I saw this coming.

When the arguing began, I kicked him to the curb and wanted nothing to do with him. I figured he had been using people like me for quite some time. Thinking I was going to help him forever and trying to make me feel guilty because I began to ignore his every wish, he began ranting and raving about every little thing. I got sick of it and told him I could no longer support him. We went our separate ways when we reached Islamabad.

I felt sorry for him, but I couldn't put up with his whining and arguing.

I quickly looked for any orange-haired hippies or junkies, as they were known, to find a place to buy another ten bottles of morphine. Between me and Tommy, we had used up nearly all ten bottles I had purchased in Lahore.

Within ten minutes, I entered a large park in the center of the city and, wandering around a large fountain, were the people I had been looking for. There were nearly a dozen or more junkies and when I approached them and asked for directions to a pharmacy that sold bottles of morphine, a young Briton with a long, dark beard and shoulder-length hair introduced himself. His name was David. He told me he was from John Lennon's town of Liverpool and had been in Pakistan for over a year to feed his drug habit. The others in the crowd, he told me, were all morphine addicts from nearly every country in Europe.

THE AGE OF AQUARIUS II

As I introduced myself to David and the crowd, the young Briton took me aside and we began walking out of the park to one of the main streets of Islamabad. He was taking me to a legal drug den for Pakistani's; however, they would turn their heads when foreigners wanted to purchase drugs. This might have been a drug den but not the drugs I was looking for.

I mentioned this to David and he stated he brought me to this place in case I wanted to buy some Pakistani hashish or opium from the Swat Valley, just South of Baluchistan, which was a neutral zone between Pakistan and Afghanistan. Once finished shopping he would take me to a pharmacy that sold as many bottles of morphine as I wanted. I smiled in appreciation and began looking over the shop's goods.

The man behind the counter pulled out a large, flat pan that contained three different types of opium and one type of hashish. I had bought that kind of hash in America.

Pakistani hashish is good but not quite as good as Afghani or Kashmiri hashish. However, I bought eight, one inch squares of the rubbery, black hash, which added up to about fifty grams and then asked about the three types of opium. As he pointed to each type, he told me that one was for eating, one for smoking, and one for shooting up. I chose the type for smoking and purchased ten grams of it. The cost: fifty rupee; about five US dollars.

The man placed my goods in a small plastic bag and handed them to me as I paid him. I then placed the drugs in my shoulder bag.

Now that my shopping was done, I followed David to the pharmacy, which was about a ten minute walk from the drug den.

I thanked David for taking me to the interesting shop and conversed about many different things while walking to the pharmacy. Once there, he introduced me to the pharmacist and I, in turn, purchased another ten bottles of my drug of choice.

As we left the pharmacy, I asked David if he knew of a cheap hotel. He did, and as we walked, we talked; about many different subjects.

The hotel he chose for me was decent and cheap. Although my room was on the roof with outside showers, I didn't mind. The days were hot and the nights just a few degrees cooler; an outside shower was a gift. I needed one badly as I began to stink due to the buildup of perspiration from my withdrawal from Methadone.

I invited David to my room where we smoked both the hash and opium. Luckily he carried a pipe in his pocket that we used eagerly. He turned down my offer to "shoot up" a few tablets of morphine. Unfortunately, he had no syringe with him and I wasn't about to let him use mine. Anyway, neither of us wanted to catch any diseases we might have had.

David stayed nearly an hour before leaving, to return the next morning so I could help him cash his travelers' checks. I didn't understand his reasoning for help. However, he helped me in my quest and I would help him if he needed it. If he intended robbing the bank, that was out of the question. I would learn that he had stolen a British passport and travelers' checks from one of his countrymen, which didn't set too well with me.

I had given my word to help him and I did. I had to vouch for him with the bank teller, telling him I was a friend of David's and that the travelers' checks and passport were his even though the picture in the stolen passport didn't quite look like him. It was hard to tell because each had a long, dark beard and long, dark hair. However, taking a closer look, there was a difference in their facial features.

We acted as though we were traveling together and I had a few travelers' checks to cash also, which would help him in his quest. As the teller looked at the picture and then at David, I mentioned that he was my friend and we were traveling together. With that, the teller happily cashed his checks. My word seemed to make all the difference.

THE AGE OF AQUARIUS II

Once done, David thanked me and wished me luck; I did the same. That was the last time I saw him.

I headed back to my hotel room where I met another guest who was Pakistani and spoke decent English.

He mentioned that tonight the television shows were in English. That shocked me that they had television.

Their northern neighboring country, Afghanistan, had none.

I returned to my room, leaving my door open during the day to catch a sometimes cool breeze; and "shoot up" without concern; that is, until my Pakistani friend peeked into my room and caught me in action. He scolded me about my actions.

I invited him in and lied, explaining that I had cancer and was using the needle only for medicinal purposes. However, he didn't believe me.

I didn't care; I was on vacation and did what I had to do to relieve my addiction.

It was getting dark and he invited me downstairs to watch television. The first show was Colombo and then Lost in Space. That was it.

I returned to my room, smoked some hash and opium using a homemade pipe I had made from a toilet paper tube and aluminum foil. It worked ok. A few puffs of each and I was in dreamland.

The next morning, after my "fix" and a bowl of cornflakes with goats' milk, I went for a walk.

Next door to the hotel was a carpet store, so I went in.

I had taken my Polaroid camera along in case I wanted to take a few shots of the city.

As I was looking through the carpets, the owner and a few of his friends were sitting around a small table having a conversation. They seemed to be interested in the blue object I had in my hand. I showed them by taking a picture.

"It's a magic camera," I told them.

Once I had taken their picture, I set it in front of them. They saw a black picture and told me that my camera didn't work. Again I mentioned that it was a magic camera and to wait a few more seconds. As they stared into the black square, suddenly the picture appeared. They had never seen anything like it in their life. Because of the humidity, Polaroid cameras weren't sold in Pakistan because most of the time the pictures would turn out cloudy or not at all. That was outside. Inside, however, it worked well.

They now believed that indeed, it WAS a "Magic Camera."

The owner wanted it at any cost and began showing me carpet after carpet. He was willing to trade me a dozen silk carpets for the camera.

I took another picture of them and again they were "flabbergasted" and couldn't believe what they had seen.

I told the owner that I would only take one carpet for the $20.00 camera. I picked out a powder blue carpet with tribal designs and handed him the camera. I promised to bring him another package of film, which I did the following morning before leaving for my trip to Peshawar.

I went to the train station and bought the ticket. Within an hour, I was well on my way to Peshawar and, hopefully, Afghanistan.

However, my dreams would fall short.

After reaching Peshawar, I went directly to the Afghan Consulate. They told me I had to get my visa in Islamabad; the place I had left a few days before.

I was very depressed. I had ridden the train for more than two days, with very little sleep and food. Now I had to return to Islamabad. I had nobody to blame but myself.

David had told me I could get my visa in Peshawar. Evidently, he was wrong. I should have asked someone at my hotel or visited the American Embassy. My stupidity had gotten me into this nightmare. Oh well, back to the capital of Pakistan.

THE AGE OF AQUARIUS II

Two hours into the trip, I had fallen asleep. When I had awakened, I reached into my bag for some money to buy a Pepsi and Kabob sandwich. Suddenly I was speechless. Someone had stolen all of my money.

I kept my money in my bag and my passport and other papers in my boot. Now I only had enough money for the trip to Kabul and maybe a week's stay in Pakistan. *This was the worst thing that could happen to me*, I thought.

But it wasn't. The Afghan Embassy refused to allow me a visa to travel in Afghanistan. Now I was really screwed. I would have to go to the American Embassy and send a wire to my parents for money and plane fare to America. My ticket from Kabul was useless. I found out weeks later that I could have turned in my ticket to Pan Am and traded it for one from Pakistan.

Although I didn't ask, the Ambassador said nothing about that when I asked him to send a wire for me. Other than that, they couldn't help me. I was well aware of that from trips I had taken in the past. I even had to pay for the wire when I received my money from my parents.

Three days later, I returned to the Embassy and received my answer. A wire transfer was waiting for me at the same bank I had been to before.

I received the money and returned to the Embassy to pay for the wire. The Ambassador then asked why my passport wasn't stolen along with my money. I quickly explained the reason. He then handed me a plane ticket to New York City. I was to take a bus to Karachi; a city that was under reconstruction to house more than a hundred thousand new tenants. It was a chance for a new life and jobs for the Pakistanis. So new, in fact, that they hadn't laid tracks for a train. That's the reason I had to ride a bus to Karachi.

New paved roads showed us the path to this new city. Once there, I only had four hours to catch my plane. It was a non-stop flight to New York, and then I would change planes for Detroit.

I carried my carpet with me and the other few gifts I bought I placed in my luggage. Many of the things I bought were from China. I got them because Chinese goods were illegal in America; or so I thought. I bought Mao Tse-Tung's Red book about his communist revolution and other little trinkets.

I also smuggled the hash, opium, and approximately one thousand half-grain tablets of pharmaceutical morphine.

I had no trouble leaving Pakistan. Customs saw that I had a carpet and other Pakistani gifts. It showed them that I was a tourist and nothing else. Little did they know?

I did, however, worry about US customs; especially when the customs inspector found my little red book. "Are you a communist?" he asked suspiciously.

"No. Why?" I retorted.

He held up the book. "This is the reason."

I looked surprised. "It's from China. You can't get things from China."

"You can buy this in any bookstore."

"Are you serious? I thought you couldn't buy goods from China," I exclaimed.

"You sure can. Can I have it?" he asked.

"No."

"Did you read it?"

"NO! I bought it because I thought you couldn't get it here?" You can tell from the binding that I hadn't even opened it." I added, "I also purchased some Nivea cream made in China. Can you buy that here too?"

"I don't know about that."

The customs man placed my little red book back in my only piece of luggage and let me pass through.

As I began to walk away, he pointed to a room in front and to the right of me and said, "Go to aisle 2 in that room over there."

I nodded and walked slowly to the room designated. I thought to myself: Here goes. Now they're going to strip search me and find my illegal contraband. But when I got there the room was empty except for a woman behind the counter of aisle 2.

"The customs man told me to come here," I told her.

"Have you been to Pakistan or India," she asked.

"Yes." She handed me a flyer about Cholera and then let me leave.

I thought for sure I was going to get busted. *I was lucky this time*, I thought to myself. I continued on my way, leaving the international customs area and into the USA heading for my flight to Detroit.

I couldn't wait to get home and have a talk with Pete about my money from our investments. He had millions of my dollars and I wanted it.

I had been cool as a cucumber going through customs with my illegal contraband. I had brought with me from Pakistan about two ounces of hash, an ounce or so of excellent opium, and all of those tablets of morphine.

Within an hour, I caught my flight to Metro Airport, which was just an hours' drive to my parent's home.

I had phoned my parents from Kennedy Airport and told them the flight I would be on so they could pick me up. They were there waiting for me. I placed my one piece of luggage into their car and we headed to their place.

After explaining the ordeal I had experienced in Pakistan, we were at their home within five minutes. It was late. We said "good night" and every one went to their bedrooms.

After taking the contraband, which I had taped to my body inside my underwear, I threw the stuff on the bed and laughed. I found a pipe in one of my drawers and smoked a little of the opium and then went into the kitchen, got a spoon and some water and took it into the bedroom. I always had a syringe hidden behind a drawer just for times when I spent the night at my parents' house. I pulled it out and "fixed" a couple of tablets. I lay back on the bed as the "rush" took over my body. I was in ecstasy.

A few minutes later, after cleaning up, I returned the syringe back to its rightful place, took the spoon and glass of water to the kitchen and then went back to my bedroom and fell asleep.

The next morning, my mom made a big breakfast: bacon, eggs, hash potatoes, French toast and orange juice.

Two hours later, my mom drove me back to my place. Once there, I called a few close friends and showed off my "goodies." They had never smoked real opium before so I turned them on to it. After a few tokes, they were soon "nodding" in their chairs. They didn't have any type of addiction, except maybe to cocaine.

Once they awoke, we smoked some of the Paki hash. They enjoyed it but told me it didn't quite have the kick of the Affy hash that I had sent to them years before. An hour later they were gone.

A few minutes later, after doing some morphine, I contacted Pete by phone. He told me to meet him at a secluded restaurant a few miles from his place. I was there within an hour.

After shaking hands I gave him a big hug and told him, "I thought I would never see you again."

He smiled and now walked with a limp. To help him steady himself he used a beautiful gold-handled, black cane.

The first thing that came out of his mouth was, "I know what you want."

"Yeah, and what, pray tell is that?"

Just as he was about to tell me, the waitress brought us some coffee.

"You want your money," he exclaimed.

I nodded. "That's what I'm here for."

"Before you say another fucking word, let me explain what happened."

"I know what happened. Your crew beat you with baseball bats and left you for dead and then placed you in your car and had a semi hit it head on."

THE AGE OF AQUARIUS II

"Where did you find that out?"

"I had my mom speak to Helen. Your wife was afraid for her life and told my mom what had happened to you. She never thought you would make it through the coma. What I've told you is between me and you. So don't get angry at Helen."

"Listen and listen good, you little shit. Don't EVER and I mean EVER tell me what and what not to do. Is that understood?"

"I'm sorry, Pete. I shouldn't have told you. You're my uncle. I mentioned this to you as your nephew, not one of your scumbags you used to call your crew."

"You're right, kid. I haven't been the same person as I used to be. But now I gotta tell you some bad news." He added, "In fact, let's get out of here and take a ride."

Oh shit, I said to myself. *He's going to take me to someplace and whack me.* "Sure, Uncle Pete."

We left the restaurant and got into a brand new Cadillac. "Nice car," I told him.

He backed out of the parking lot and floored the accelerator, the back tires throwing rocks and dust yards behind the car.

He began explaining what had happened to him and my money. I knew I was about to hear some bad news. This news, however, made me sick to my stomach.

"When I finally got out of the hospital, Helen and I, along with my two daughters, stayed at her sister's house because I was concerned for my family. I took Helen, Helena and Jennifer. Their lives were in danger. So was yours, but I couldn't find you. Your mom said you were moving from house to house because you were afraid that my crew would do to you what they did to me. You were a liability to them. You've got some balls, kid. If you had been born Sicilian, I would have opened the books and made you a member of La Cosa Nostra. But FUCK that! Both of us were liabilities. Once I began getting stronger and had the use of my legs, I had a 'friend of a friend' get in touch with the 'powers that be' and asked them for a 'sit-down.' I knew I was taking a chance and could take a bullet in the head, but I had to take the chance. I didn't care what happened to me. I was doing it for my family."

"Where do I come into this?"

"Shut the fuck up and I'll get to you," he bellowed, giving me a dirty look.

I stared out the front window. At that moment I didn't want to be there. "I'm sorry," I whispered.

"Because I didn't do the hit on Hoffa as ordered, my crew set me up, ordered by my old friend and boss, Giacalone. When they found out that I wasn't dead, Giacalone was furious and ordered the death of three of my crew. They haven't been seen since. But I heard Sal and Louie had their tongues cut out, before they were shot in the head."

He went on telling me that his meeting was with his boss, Giacalone, and his Godfather, Don Tocco. Pete wanted a new start and pleaded with them for both his and my life. The powers that be talked it over amongst themselves and ordered Pete to give up all his money and investments, including the money he and I had made from my hash deal, which was worth millions: MY MILLIONS. If he agreed, he would be allowed to stay a "capo," recruit a new crew, and stay as a Union Delegate in the Painter's Union. He would be given the job as arbitrator, deciding which local would get a particular job, such as painting the Mackinaw or Windsor Bridge. He would wield a lot of power.

For this, Pete and I and our families would be allowed to live.

There was nothing I could do about this. I had to suck it up and not think about the millions of dollars I had lost by investing in Pete's deals. All my work and heartache from my hash deal and I ended up with nothing but a story to tell: So much for my dreams.

Thank God my Dad taught me the tool and die business. Now I'd have to go out and get a real job to make an honest day's wage. My leadership qualities and knowledge in the tool and die trade would have to suffice. I was finished with drug dealing for good. I would no longer have to look over my shoulder.

Maybe losing all of that money taught me a lesson. Smuggling and dealing drugs would no longer be part of my life. I was through with that for GOOD!

May God have mercy on my soul?

The End.

www.ingramcontent.com/pod-product-compliance
Lightning Source LLC
Chambersburg PA
CBHW031250290426
44109CB00012B/513